The Refle...

The Reflective Leader

Standing Still to Move Forward

Alan Smith
and Peter Shaw

CANTERBURY
PRESS
Norwich

© Alan Smith and Peter Shaw 2011

First published in 2011 by the Canterbury Press Norwich
Editorial office
13–17 Long Lane,
London, EC1A 9PN, UK

Canterbury Press is an imprint of Hymns Ancient and Modern Ltd
(a registered charity)
13A Hellesdon Park Road, Norwich,
Norfolk, NR6 5DR, UK

www.scmcanterburypress.co.uk

British Library Cataloguing in Publication data

A catalogue record for this book is available
from the British Library

978 1 84825 083 3

Typeset by Regent Typesetting, London
Printed and bound in Great Britain by
CPI William Clowes, Beccles, Suffolk

Contents

Acknowledgements ix

Foreword by the Archbishop of York xi

Introduction xiii

Part One　Know yourself 1

  1　Know what you are trying to do 3

  2　Know your values 7

  3　Know what motivates you 11

  4　Know your strengths 15

  5　Know your weaknesses 19

  6　Know your default behaviours 23

  7　Know how to reflect 27

Part Two　Understand others 31

  8　The importance of understanding others 33

  9　The importance of nurturing the best in others 37

10　The importance of building common purpose 41

11　The importance of listening 44

12　The importance of feedback 48

13　The importance of keeping an open mind 51

14　The importance of a good crisis 55

Part Three   Create a flourishing team   59

15 Create a positive team   61
16 Create space for reflection   65
17 Create a coaching culture   69
18 Create a culture where dissenting voices can be
    heard   73
19 Create a positive culture   77
20 Create the capacity to make decisions   81
21 Create a culture of celebration   85

Part Four   Read the context   89

22 Maintain the balance between knowledge and
    wisdom   91
23 Maintain the balance between the urgent and
    the important   94
24 Maintain the balance between understanding
    threats and taking risks   98
25 Maintain the balance between the ideal and the
    pragmatic   102
26 Maintain the balance between uncertainty and
    clarity   106
27 Maintain the balance between giving clear
    direction and willingness to change   110
28 Maintain the balance between giving a lead
    and enabling others to take the lead   114

Part Five   Next steps   119

29 What happens when you stand and stare?   121
30 What lights your fire?   125
31 Who are your companions on the way?   128

Postscript   131

Other Books written by Alan Smith and Peter Shaw 132

To
John Waller and John Townroe,
and David Quine and Judy Brown,
who have enabled us to reflect along
our respective life journeys

Acknowledgements

We want to thank those who have helped us reflect both as leaders and in our work with leaders. Alan is particularly grateful for the encouragement from the teams he worked with in the Dioceses of Lichfield and St Albans. Peter is very appreciative of the wisdom and encouragement of his colleagues at Praesta Partners.

We first met in 2005 and have enjoyed rewarding and stimulating conversations over the last few years. We bring together varied experiences and approaches having worked in different spheres. Together in this book we focus on the importance of leadership and the need to grow and nurture leaders in demanding times.

We believe that the art of reflection is a crucial aspect of leadership. We both come from a Christian heritage. Our intent is to draw on the tradition of spiritual wisdom and the best of good practice from those leaders who have been able to combine activity and reflection successfully.

We are grateful to those who have read the book in draft and provided valuable comments. In particular, we would like to acknowledge the contribution of Ian Jones, Hilary Fairfield, Andy Piggott, Alan Harvey, Zoe Stear and David Brockman.

Christine Smith has been an admirable editor. She has supported us as we developed the ideas for the book and has made some helpful suggestions. We are grateful to Helen Burtenshaw and Mary Handford who have managed our diaries so we have been able to meet and reflect on the themes in the book. We thank Jackie Tookey for her practical help with some of the typing. Helen Burtenshaw has shown great patience in linking together some of our disparate contributions into one complete text.

Peter's wife, Frances, has been a source of both teasing and encouragement. She regards both of us as activists rather than reflectors and finds it amusing that we should be writing a book on the reflective leader. Our justification is that because we are activists by nature, we are still learning how to reflect. We are not exemplars of reflection: we are learning.

We are delighted that John Sentamu has written the Foreword. John is an inspiration as someone who has given a strong lead in a variety of contexts: as a young lawyer when he opposed Idi Amin in Uganda and was arrested; later, when he was Bishop of Stepney and chaired the Damiola Taylor review; and now as Archbishop of York.

All our royalties for the book are going to the Bishop of St Albans Community Development Fund.

We hope that the book will stimulate thought and encourage some practical reflection as you develop different approaches in your journey as a leader.

Foreword

Reflection is at the heart of my life and work as an archbishop. I am privileged to meet a wide range of people in many different situations: listening, encouraging, sharing and challenging. It would be possible to fill my day ten times over with interesting and worthwhile activity. This makes the discipline of reflection a necessity, not an option. I need to stand back regularly and place my experiences and observations in a wider perspective. I have to look beyond my immediate busyness and reflect on my own journey lest I get swept along by a tide of trivia, and the seduction of what others see as urgent. Benign neglect is a great antidote. Taking time out to reflect sharpens my understanding of individuals and situations. It enables me to understand better the complex human, political, economic and religious context that I find myself operating in.

We live in a time of rapid change. The turbulence that many people are experiencing can generate huge pressure on priorities. Making adequate space for reflection can easily become a casualty of an overfull diary. But quality reflection is not escapism or romanticism. It is crucial to good leadership. It reminds us of our values and encourages us to live them. It creates an internal space in which we become clearer about the contribution we can make in a given situation. This is how a leader can make a difference.

In this book Alan Smith and Peter Shaw have combined the best of good management practice with spiritual wisdom and insight. Their approach is practical and easy to follow, with questions to consider at the end of each chapter. They are an unusual joint authorship. Alan was Bishop of Shrewsbury before becoming the Diocesan Bishop of St Albans. Peter was a director general within the UK Government before becoming an executive coach and a business school professor in leadership development. Peter brings the practical insights you would expect of a Reader or Licensed Lay Minister, with nearly 40 years' experience of working with those in leadership positions. Alan brings a lifetime of leadership not only in the Church, but from chairing regional bodies such as the Shropshire Strategic Partnership.

This book is not convoluted theory. Its chapters are realistic, robust and relevant. Whether you are leading two people or two hundred, whether they are employees or volunteers, you will find these reflections engaging and challenging. Be ready to stand still to move forward. Be open to your own reflections as you read on. May it stimulate you into a quality of activity which makes the biggest difference for good.

Dr John Sentamu
Archbishop of York

Introduction

Reflection is essential for effective leadership. To be reflective is to be curious and to ask how others view the issues we are confronting. It is about seeing the bigger picture, focusing on the longer term, and always bringing a wider perspective to bear. Prioritizing time for reflection is not a selfish indulgence. It is about ensuring the most demanding issues are addressed and that problems are not ignored.

Reflection is about legitimizing thinking time. Rapid pace of change, pressure from the media for instant comments, the risk of emotional overreaction and the loss of organizational experience and wisdom are all reasons why in the contemporary world leaders need more time to reflect, not less.

Each of us reflects in different ways. For some, wide reading is an essential element or the intentional creation of periods of silence. Some imagine what it is to stand in someone else's shoes, consciously allowing time for in-depth discussion, or working in a reflective way with a coach.

The importance of reflection

The title of this book is deliberately ambiguous. We chose *The Reflective Leader* because, at its most basic level, leadership is not just about the things we do or the techniques we use. The most fundamental factor that affects our leadership is who we are: our values, our character, our attitudes and our personality. In this book we argue that who we are as leaders is just as important as what we do. Character is as essential as skills.

The book title also suggests that one of the crucial habits that leaders need to develop is reflection – about ourselves, about others and about the context in which we are operating. Without systematic reflection individuals and organizations can quickly lose sight of what they are doing and its impact. For the physical and mental well-being of those who work in the organization, as well as its long-term flourishing, time for reflection is crucial.

The West Wing is a fast-moving television series about the President of the United States of America and the team that works around him. It portrays a president who makes decisions in seconds, often about matters which have world-wide repercussions. He is constantly on the move. Many of the decisions seem to be made as he walks in the corridors between meetings while having rapid conversations with his assistants. He is a man of action. He knows what needs to be done and makes snap decisions on the hoof. It makes gripping drama, but it underplays a vital part of leadership: the time and discipline required for reflection.

Good leaders have a sound grasp of the factors that impact on their organization. They are shrewd judges of character and make well-considered appointments. They understand the wide range of issues that might influence what they are trying to achieve. They are able to read what is going on in the wider society or in their market. They spot emerging trends and opportunities. Some do it instinctively, while others do it because they are widely read, they are in touch with other people working in the same area and they are able to draw relevant information together to make considered decisions. They are leaders who have learnt how to reflect.

This book looks at how leaders, in the midst of their busy working lives, can develop the habit of reflection and how this capacity to reflect can make a tangible difference to the flourishing of an organization.

The writer H. G. Wells reportedly said most individuals only think once or twice in a lifetime. In contrast, he claimed that he had made an international reputation by thinking once or twice a year. Getting into the habit of reflecting is not straightforward. It is easier to go along with the myths that my group has about itself and not face up to hard truths about the organization we are leading or are part of.

Honest reflection is time consuming, costly and challenging. The opportunity for reflection is essential for everyone within an organization. But it is especially important for those responsible for its overall direction and its culture. A vital part of a leader's responsibility is to create an organization that values and practises the habit of reflection so that everyone can contribute to its flourishing.

The cost of short-termism

According to Craig Mundie, Microsoft chief research and strategy officer, 'A great many companies have a fairly short lifespan. Even many big, great companies only last thirty years or so.' Who would have thought that Woolworths, which was such a familiar sight on every high street in the United Kingdom, would have collapsed so suddenly?

It is significant that most business leaders are in post for just a few years. Boards of large organizations are impatient and are always looking for the one great leader who can help them grow and outperform their competitors. Many leaders are unceremoniously replaced the moment the organization goes through a bad patch. This is a phenomenon that is all too familiar to managers of professional football teams.

Why do so few organizations survive for long periods and why do many leaders stay in post for a short time? Part of the answer is that leaders are under such pressure to 'do' that they do not have enough time and space to reflect. Do they have time to look to previous experience and to understand some of the age-old insights about human nature, and how people can work together successfully?

In his book *The Defence of the Realm* (Penguin, 2010), Christopher Andrews, professor of modern and contemporary history at Cambridge University, describes a phenomenon called, 'Historical Attention Span Deficit Syndrome' (HASDS). 'Short-termism', he says, 'has been the distinguishing intellectual vice of our age. For the first time in recorded history, there has been a widespread assumption that the experience of all previous generations is irrelevant to present policy' (p. 585). Andrews attributes the banking crisis which broke in 2008 at least in part to this 'syndrome'. We thought we had little to learn from the past. We kidded ourselves that in this brave new world of economic expansion we could never experience the sort of financial crises that our grandparents had to endure. How wrong we were.

Drawing on insights from the past

It is here that leaders can benefit from drawing on the spiritual and monastic wisdom which has been the foundation of so much of the progress in the Western world. In the medieval period there were two texts about leadership which were of supreme importance: the *Rule* of St Benedict and the *Pastoral Rule* of St Gregory the Great. They summarize centuries of distilled wisdom about how human beings can organize their life together and how leadership might be best exercised. These texts still pose penetrating questions about how we exercise leadership today. For example, Gregory identified two qualities above all others that are vital for a leader. First, he wrote about 'contemplation before action', which is the theme of this book. Second, he pointed to service. Those leaders who think that their individual actions are the most important factor in an organization are kidding themselves. What is required is someone who serves the organization so that it flourishes and grows.

We draw from these sources of ancient wisdom, along with contemporary insights, to help leaders think about their core values and to develop the practice of regular reflection.

The structure of this book

We have sought to make the book relevant to you whether you are leading two people or two hundred people. You might be responsible for employees or volunteers. The organization you work in might be in the private, public or voluntary sectors. It might be a company, a charity, a church or a prison.

This book explores reflection in four key areas, namely:

- Know yourself. Be clear what you are trying to achieve. Identify your core values and motivations. How can you build on your strengths and compensate for your limitations?
- How can we understand others better? What motivates us? What paralyses us?
- How can we enable teams to flourish? How do we help teams grow and excel?
- How can we read the context more accurately? In a changing world, how do we keep abreast of what is going on?

Each of the 31 chapters ends with questions. Many of these touch on our deepest values and motivations. We suggest that as you work through the chapters of the book, you give time to mull over the questions. You may find it helpful to read it at the same time as a colleague, so that you have someone else with whom you can discuss the ideas and who will help you work through your own responses. The book can be used to provide a reflection a day over a month. You may wish to read it again a year later and revisit the same questions to see what changes have been made.

We hope that this book will be a means of enabling you to grow in self-knowledge and understanding as you develop the vital discipline of reflection.

PART ONE

Know yourself

One of the most fundamental questions for any leader is 'How well do I know myself?' Understanding ourselves well can create stability and calmness. It enables us to be less thrown by the events of the week. Accepting ourselves for who we are, warts and all, provides an essential starting point on the journey to become a measured and reflective leader.

Part One suggests that we need to be clear about what we are trying to achieve and about the importance of our values. We need to know what motivates us, to identify our strengths, to compensate for our weaknesses and to acknowledge our default behaviours.

It concludes with some practical suggestions about how to reflect more effectively. We hope this will stimulate you to develop sources of reflection that work well for you.

Know what you are trying to do

Stephanie's predecessor, Bill, was known as someone who led from the front. While some considered Bill to be dynamic, others experienced him as dominating and felt that he did not listen to their opinions. There was not much discussion about future direction. Bill expected his staff to implement his decisions with little debate.

Stephanie had been surprised and delighted by her meteoric rise to lead the organization. Her colleagues agreed that she was immensely able and most of them were genuinely excited by her appointment. Her first step was to call together her team and explain that she wanted to work with them to build a vision for the whole organization and to grow it.

She asked each of them to provide a brief report on the trends of the previous five years. They spent time together analysing the factors that were impinging on their work. From this mass of data they then worked on building a consensus on the way forward. They distilled this into six statements that described what they were trying to achieve. From this they devised the strategy that undergirded the rapid growth of the organization. Once agreed, Stephanie found she did not have to persuade her colleagues to implement the new strategy. Having been involved in developing it, they were already fully committed to it.

It sounds an obvious thing to ask, but do you know what you are setting out to do? If asked, can you summarize what you want to do and how you hope to achieve it? Are you clear about the underlying trends affecting your organization which you either need to build on or counter? Can you identify the main threats to its thriving that you have to overcome?

This can be more challenging than it sounds as the leader needs to hold the overall vision ('We want to support as many homeless people as possible') as well as the strategy of how to get there ('We are going to open another homeless centre before the end of the year'). The strategy then needs to be broken down into a series of aims which are crucial if the strategy is going to be delivered ('We have to increase the number of donors to fund the new centre', 'We need to recruit someone to lead the project' and 'We have to identify and train thirty volunteers by September'). Although the overall vision may stay the same, the strategy and the aims will change over time.

Some leaders have little grasp of what they are trying to do or how they are planning to achieve it. If the leader is not clear then no one else in the organization is likely to have much clarity either. Worse still, colleagues may hold subtly conflicting views that have never been articulated but which work against the organization succeeding. One of the features of most growing organizations is that not only is the leader articulate about what they are doing but that they have built a team and a workforce which also knows where they are going and how they expect to get there.

Some think that the role of the leader is to devise the vision, the strategy and the aims and then tell everyone else in the organization what they are. It is true that one role of the leader is to ensure that there is a common vision, strategy and aims. However they should not feel that they have to produce these alone. There are few leaders who are so omnicompetent that they understand all the external factors and internal processes which impinge upon the organization. How much better to engage everyone's creative energies and ideas at the earliest stage to really understand what is happening both in the organization and in the wider context. This can then become the basis of future plans which are much more likely to succeed if everyone has already worked on them together.

There is another problem when a leader decides the vision, strategy and aims and then tells their colleagues what they are. Telling people something does not mean that others will necessarily implement it enthusiastically. Indeed, persuading others to adopt a vision and a strategy may involve a great deal of time explaining what they are and why they should adopt them. Generally it is more effective and much quicker to involve our colleagues at the earliest stage. Having been consulted and engaged in the process, they will understand the reasons for it and why it is better than the alternatives.

Once the broad strategy has been agreed, the leader has to be careful not to get bogged down in micromanagement. This is a fine judgement to be made here. Some details of an organization's work need watching very carefully as they could threaten the overall success. But there will be other areas where we need to trust our colleagues to work out the best way of implementing the strategy. If the overall leader decides every last detail they are likely to disempower colleagues and create a dependent culture which stifles creativity and the taking of responsibility.

One thoughtful leader makes a distinction between principles and preferences. He argues that we need to be very clear about the fundamental issues and the guiding principles of our work. These are non negotiable. However, there are other areas which he calls preferences, where people can be given freedom to get on with the job in the way that they see fit.

For reflection

- Can you articulate succinctly the overall vision of your organization?
- What are the three most important aims of your organization that will deliver the strategy?

- Does everyone in your organization know what they are? If they do not, what are you going to do to share them?
- Does everyone know their part in implementing the vision, strategy and aims?

2

Know your values

Angela started work as a solicitor in a Midlands city in the 1970s. In her first few months she was disconcerted that several clients asked her to do things that she considered unethical. She was clear she would never do anything dishonest or immoral. As a result she lost several clients, much to the criticism of a colleague who was eager to build up the firm's business as quickly as possible.

She recounts the day when a well-known businessman stomped out of her office angrily, saying that she was naive and needed to be more 'flexible'. For several years she struggled to build up her client base, but gradually her reputation as a woman who had high principles won over. Looking back, she believes that the growth of her firm (she is now the senior partner) is not just because they are good at their work, but is also due to their reputation for integrity.

Most of us want to work for an organization we can be proud of. We would like it to have an excellent reputation and be renowned for its positive ethos and values. However, the way that we maintain the highest values is by the leader embodying and practising them, relentlessly and consistently.

How do we develop a workforce that is passionate about what we are doing? How do we become known as an organization that treats its employees and customers well? No amount of management technique or spin will suffice. The key way such changes come about is through a leader who lives out these positive values day by day. As Leo Tolstoy was reputed to have said, 'Everyone thinks of changing the world, but no one thinks of changing himself.'

Most employees or volunteers look for a leader who they can respect and emulate. It sounds rather old fashioned, but they want people who lead by example. Here the age-old maxim, found in various forms in all the world's main religions, holds true: Do unto others as you would have them do unto you. Or to put it in another of its popular forms: Treat others as you want to be treated.

Most of us instinctively have an innate sense of fairness. We can spot a leader who has double standards and who grabs everything they can get. When a leader complains that the workforce is only interested in what they can take out of the organization, the first thing they need to do is to look at themselves. Do the employees or volunteers see a leader who believes so much in what the organization is doing that they are prepared to make sacrifices? Is the leader recognized as someone who is giving all their energies and passions to it? Perhaps all they see is a leader only interested in the perks. Many of us are willing to work sacrificially, often way beyond the hours that are expected, when we believe in the worth of what we are doing.

Or take another feature of many successful organizations: loyalty. How do we hold onto good employees or volunteers in a competitive market? Beyond a certain level of remuneration we cannot buy loyalty. If employees or volunteers are treated as if they are dispensable ('I'm the boss and if you don't want to do it my way then leave'), then they are not going to be loyal when we are going through difficult times. What builds loyalty is a leader who is loyal.

The most important resource in any organization is the staff or volunteers. When people discuss how they want to be treated, high on the list is that we want to matter for who we are, not just for what we do. We want our views to be respected, our contribution to be valued and to be treated fairly. These are deep human aspirations that transcend time, class, religion and gender. Where mutual respect is taken seriously in an organization, most people will be set free to give of their best. Conversely when an organization treats people as dispensable, where suggestions are rubbished and favouritism is rife, many employees do the minimum required.

The leader sets the standards of the organization. There are several areas in which this is important. For example, it does not take staff or volunteers long to discover if the leader is untruthful. When the leader asks someone to tell a lie, even if it is about something unimportant, it may resolve a difficult situation in the short term. But from then on it is known that it is all right to be economical with the truth. If it is acceptable to be untruthful to someone outside the organization, then why not to each other?

Another area is gossip. Some leaders are renowned for talking about their colleagues behind their backs in unflattering terms. Not only are their abilities mocked but even their motivations are called into question. Often done with humour this may be superficially amusing and can be flattering to those in the leader's 'in group'.

However, if we know that the boss is someone who talks about others behind their backs, would we go to them when we are worried about something? Probably not, because we know that the leader is the sort of person who cannot keep confidences and who does not respect colleagues. Instead of creating a culture where everyone is open about their gifts and weaknesses and where there is a willingness to learn, gossip divides and demotivates.

How do we respond when someone is critical about a colleague behind their back? Do we ignore it, thereby creating a culture which is fundamentally dishonest or do we discuss the problems with them? Not only is there a possibility that this might improve the situation, but it sends out a message that the mature way to deal with frustrations is to talk them through. The complainer also picks up the subliminal message that if we are unhappy with their work we will discuss it with them, not say disparaging things behind their back.

In terms of honesty, is the leader known to treat employees

fairly or do they routinely presume upon their employees to work beyond what is expected? Do they use their position of power to get what they want, knowing that some employees respond out of fear of being passed over? This sort of honesty is just as important as the leader being seen to be scrupulous when it comes to expenses and perks. When the leader acts with honesty and integrity, it encourages a culture where honesty and integrity is valued throughout the organization.

For reflection

- How would your colleagues describe your values and attitudes? To what extent do you exemplify the values that you want others in the organization to hold?
- List the ways in which you want to be treated by others in the organization. Are these the values with which you treat others?
- How can we encourage a culture of openness where we talk to each other face-to-face rather than behind others' backs?
- How have you demonstrated loyalty to colleagues in the past month?

3

Know what motivates you

We all see our work in different ways. There is the well-known story about a visitor to a building site watching three people at work, carving stone. Outwardly they all appeared to be doing exactly the same thing. The visitor paused and asked what they were doing.

'Me?' said one, 'I'm chipping away at these stones with a chisel.'

'Me?' said another, 'I'm earning my living. I get fifteen pounds an hour.'

'Me?' said the third, 'I'm building a cathedral.'

Most inspirational leaders are motivated by a great idea or ideal, which others instinctively recognize and want to be part of. Leaders need to ask themselves, 'What really motivates me? What makes me jump out of bed in the morning and inspires me to face the day with energy and passion?' For some people work will not feature high on their list. They might answer by saying that they want to earn enough money to go on holiday. Others might want to get a degree or run the marathon. These are all perfectly good ambitions but they are probably not the things that we would want to be remembered for in posterity.

Knowing our deepest motivations is important if we are going to lead with integrity and inspire others to follow. Many great leaders are individuals who have seen beyond the superficial and are motivated by ideals that others instinctively know are things that truly matter in life.

In his *Spiritual Exercises,* Ignatius Loyola helped people discern the deepest motivations in their lives. It might seem a morbid thing to do, but he asked them to imagine that they had died and to write their epitaph. If we had to compose a phrase, in no more than eight words, to sum up who we were and what we had done in our lives, what would it say? I imagine it would not be about where we went on holiday or our qualifications. It is more likely to be about the sort of person we were ('honest and caring . . .') or how others related to us ('greatly loved . . .') or the impact we had on others ('admired for . . .' or 'inspired many people to . . .'). These are some of the core qualities that make us into the person we are or would like to be. They can also have a profound influence on how we work and how we treat others now.

A second example comes from St Benedict. He says that at each of the three stages when a monk is joining the community he is asked the question, 'What is it you seek?' It may seem a ridiculous thing to ask. Surely, the answer is obvious: he wants to join the community. But Benedict is asking about the seeker's most fundamental motivations. He knows that ultimately the only thing that will sustain someone in a religious community is the longing for God. Does the person only want to belong to a community so that they would be clothed and fed? Benedict knew that he had to dig into the deepest levels of a person's desire if they were going to thrive in the community.

So what really motivates me? It is possible for us to go through life without answering that most basic of questions or to do so superficially. Some individuals do not get beyond the surface level, so they think that the most important goal in life is getting richer, finding the perfect partner or being promoted. You might sum these up as the desire for money, sex or power respectively. In Christian teaching these are the three greatest temptations. There is nothing wrong with these things in themselves as long as we use them for the good of others and we do not kid ourselves that they can give us the deepest experience of satisfaction and ultimate meaning that all human beings seek.

One of the most formative experiences of Michael's ministry was being called to a house in Reading where a woman had just died. He met her husband, a well-known local business-man, who ushered him into a huge drawing room, complete with a concert grand piano. As they talked he could see the gardener mowing the extensive lawns which stretched into the distance. The bereaved man spoke of his life and how he had built up a business from scratch, working seven days a week to provide for his family. He had always thought that when he retired he would be able to enjoy their company. His daughters had grown up and married and now, having retired four months previously, his wife had unexpectedly died. 'You see,' he said, 'I have everything that I could possibly need but now my wife has died, I no longer have any of the things that I really want.'

During the horrific events that took place in America on 9/11, many of the recorded messages that people left for their loved ones, as the plane on which they were flying was about to crash, have survived. What is significant is that no one spoke about finance or promotion. They spoke about love and relationships. They focused on the things that mattered most deeply to them.

So as leaders we need to dig into our psyches and unearth the things that truly make life worth living for us. If we under-take our work in the light of these motivations, we are much more likely to be transparent and authentic. There is a greater likelihood that we will find fulfilment in the things that really matter, rather than in the attractive yet transitory things that can so easily distract us.

This may take time and a great deal of reflection. Few indi-viduals will be motivated for a lifetime by an aim such as 'We want to make a bigger profit than last year' or 'We want to outperform our main competitor'. Conversely people are more likely to be inspired by aims such as 'We want to build a car which pollutes less' or 'We want to make a tangible improvement to the lives of those who suffer from Parkinson's disease' or 'We want to offer the very best service possible so that . . .' Finding and articulating inspiring aims is a vital part of leadership.

For reflection

- Make a list of what inspires and motivates you. Focus on the ones that relate to what you really want in life. Does your use of time and your priorities reflect these?
- Do the aims and objectives of your organization resonate with what inspires and motivates you?
- How might your use of time and your priorities better reflect what matters most to you?

4

Know your strengths

Jeremy had founded an organization to help gardeners sell their produce in local markets. Initially it had been a great success. He had collected the produce, rented the stalls, sold the vegetables and completed the paperwork. As the business grew he found that he was so busy that he could not always fill in all the paperwork. It took increasingly long periods for the gardeners and suppliers to be paid. Grumbles broke out into open criticism. Jeremy was hurt at the comments and wondered whether to pack it all in.

Simon, an old friend, heard about the frustrations and rang Jeremy, offering to talk it through. He was aware of both Jeremy's drive and his lack of organizational skills. He sought to persuade him to concentrate on what he was good at – collecting the produce and selling it – and to appoint someone to do the organizing. At first Jeremy was reluctant. After all, it had been his idea and he had developed it. Eventually, Jeremy had to admit to himself that he was not the person to expand the business.

Jeremy now acknowledges that it is a relief that he is doing the things he really likes and at which he excels. Six years on, the whole enterprise has expanded significantly. A manager is responsible for the organization and several other growers are also selling the produce in markets across the county.

Most of us think that we have a high degree of self-awareness. We reckon that we know what we are like. Because most of us in leadership roles are self-confident people (by virtue of having got to this point) there can be a tendency for us to overestimate our strengths and abilities. Having realistic self-knowledge is essential for good leadership. We need an honest assessment of our values and motivations, as well as our gifts and weaknesses. If we think that we are stronger in some area of leadership than is actually the case, we may not be able to achieve what we set out to do. We may not realize that we have to work on these areas to develop them. We may fail to appoint colleagues whose skills complement our own. On the other hand if we think we are weaker in some areas than is actually the case we may be overcautious.

We need to have a realistic estimate of our strengths, so we can build on them and develop them. But how can we grow in such self-awareness? It is a challenge for those in positions of leadership to get clear feedback. Employees in the organization know that they depend on us for promotion or for this year's bonus. If asked directly they are likely to be overgenerous in praise of our strengths and less than forthcoming about our weaknesses.

One of the greatest problems for any leader is finding colleagues whose judgement we can trust and who are willing to be open with us about our abilities. Sadly, we are more likely to be surrounded by people who say what they think we want to hear rather than what they and their colleagues truly believe. For most employees or volunteers it is simply too much hassle and involves too many risks to be honest with their boss. The result is an unhealthy collusion which helps no one. Unfortunately the higher up an organization we are, the harder it is to find someone to be open with about our strengths and weaknesses.

A wise leader will always be on the lookout for that small number of thoughtful people in the organization who can give them genuine feedback. This is not always easy, as some may be critical because they are jealous or have a chip on their shoulder. How can we find those who will genuinely try to be objective? Such individuals are a rare commodity. Often they are near retirement and know that they are not going to get promoted any further. They have seen a number of leaders come and go and they are sufficiently wise (and at peace with themselves) to dare to be honest if given the opportunity. They are a most valuable gift to any leader who wants to grow in self-knowledge.

If we cannot find such a person within the organization, then we can bring someone in from outside to listen with a constructively critical ear to help us grow in self-awareness. People are far more likely to be honest about our gifts and weaknesses when they know that the comments will be fed back anonymously through a third party.

Another way in which we can grow in self-knowledge is through work appraisals or reviews. Many organizations have a system of annual reviews although sometimes these are only for those in less senior roles. However, appraisals or reviews are more likely to be effective if everyone in the organization believes in them enough to use the system. Indeed, the best way for such schemes to be introduced is for the leaders to be the first to go through it.

Reviews for the leaders may well be conducted by someone from outside the organization or a chair of the board. It is vital that all appraisals, including the leader's, has a mechanism for an anonymous 360° feedback, from people working at different levels in the organization. Unless we are willing to be seen to learn about our strengths and weaknesses why should we expect others to be open about theirs?

Part of the challenge is to create a culture in the organization where we are honest about one another's gifts and weaknesses, so we can deploy our diverse skills and abilities in the most effective way. While it may appear to be a risky thing to do, the wise leader does not shy from such insights but instead sees them as useful information. If everyone knows that the leader is prepared to receive feedback, they are more likely to do the same.

For reflection

- What are your strengths and how do you know they are your strengths? Are you using them effectively?
- How and where do you receive feedback about the way that you lead?
- How do others in the organization know that you are learning from the feedback and responding to it?
- Who can you trust to be really honest with you? Are you doing enough to bring these people into your confidence?

5

Know your weaknesses

Jo was constantly frustrated. She was a natural visionary, who could see how the business could develop. She would dream up a new idea before breakfast nearly every day. Her colleagues used to dread her arriving at work with yet more brilliant schemes, while they were trying to implement the plans that she had brought in the previous week. The big problem was that her ideas seldom came to fruition.

Jo took some of her colleagues away for a day to talk about the future. She told them about her frustration that she was making so little progress. Jo already knew that her ability to have big ideas was one of her strengths. However, her colleagues helped her see that she had two major weaknesses.

First she was hopeless at prioritizing. Her daily bright ideas were exhausting her colleagues and dissipating their energies. She needed to work with them to sift her creative ideas and agree on the one or two that were really going to make a difference that year. She had to learn to keep quiet about all the other creative ideas that were swilling around in her head continually.

Second, she had to acknowledge that she was an ideas person, not an implementer. She needed colleagues who could think through the implications of her ideas. As a result she appointed a colleague who, when he had been given a task to do, had the talent and ability to work out how to implement it.

It is more pleasurable to explore my strengths than to have my weaknesses exposed. Yet it is a leader's weaknesses that can have the most devastating results for an organization. We can all think of individuals whose uncontrollable temper has resulted in good people resigning rather than be bullied; or the leader who can never take a difficult decision if it means they are going to be unpopular; or the person who decides to employ someone not on ability but because they like them. There are also leaders who have an inbuilt need to appoint people who will always be relied upon to say what they want to hear.

All of us have weaknesses. The difference between a good leader and a poor leader is that the good leader knows their weaknesses and does not allow them to dominate. Instead they think carefully about the extent to which they can develop their skills and abilities in their areas of weakness. They are also willing to appoint strong people around them who have the gifts to compensate for their weaknesses. They build a team which brings in the strengths that the organization needs.

But there is also a more fundamental point here. Few of us enjoy working with someone who is so competent that they know how to do everyone else's job. Such individuals leave us feeling as if we are not really needed. We wonder if we have a role in the organization. Of course, in reality there are very few people who are truly omnicompetent (only those who kid themselves that they are).

Gregory the Great, writing in the sixth century, speaks of two dangers for a leader. One is that they 'seek to be loved by their people more than they seek truth'. He notes that for some leaders the desire to be liked by others prevents them taking unpleasant decisions. This may be fatal for the long-term thriving of any organization. The second danger is that they bully and 'terrify them into submission'. Such bullying may get things done in the short term but eventually the best, most highly motivated people will move to another organization and we will be left with a weakened team.

Good leaders are those who are sufficiently secure enough in who they are that they can be honest about their weaknesses. They are strong enough to know they have to build a team which compensates for their weaknesses.

One of the most common weaknesses for a leader is the inability to change the way they work as their responsibilities grow. Early in their working life they may have been successful because they were hands-on. But if they continue to attend to the daily minutiae they will not undertake the essential planning and oversight for the long-term growth of the organization. They have to trust others to do the things that they used to enjoy doing. Instead, they have to keep focused on the big picture. They have to delegate tasks to colleagues and not interfere. This transition takes courage, self-knowledge and determination.

Some leaders fail to adjust their working style to fit their age and experience. Few people in their fifties have the same amount of raw energy they had in their twenties. Conversely, if you have been learning and reflecting you should have a great deal more insight and wisdom in your fifties than when you were in your twenties. Some leaders confuse energy and wisdom. They try to keep working with the energy of a 20-year-old when what the organization requires from them are the insights from a lifetime of experience.

Another danger for a leader is to be constantly overtired so that when a crisis hits they have no spare energy to react in a calm, collected way, drawing on their years of wisdom. Good leaders ensure they have surplus capacity to work for the long-term thriving of the organization when the going is tough.

In the first two chapters we suggested that if we want positive attitudes and values to be the hallmark of our organization then we have to embody them. Conversely, the same is true. If we are driven, we are likely to create an organization where people feel driven. If we are full of anxiety, this will seep out to others who will pick up our anxiety and feed off it.

For reflection

- What are the weaknesses which you struggle with most? Who can you trust to have an honest conversation about them?
- How are you going to compensate for them in the organization or team you lead?
- How can you adjust your way of working to take account of your energy and your experience at this stage of your life?

6

Know your default behaviours

John had started his company from scratch, working from his garage and an office in his house. Now, after 20 years, it was employing 23 full-time people and a number of part timers. It had premises on a business park. Like many small companies, margins were tight and on several occasions the business had nearly collapsed.

Those employees who had been with him for a long time knew that whenever things were difficult John would always react in the same way. He would work longer and longer hours and would check up on his colleagues incessantly. Not only was this distracting but it was perceived that he did not think his colleagues capable of doing their jobs.

Some leaders are surprisingly lacking in self-awareness and self-knowledge. It can be easier, and superficially more appealing, to live with our myths about the way our organization is or the way that leaders have to behave than to take control and change them. We all live with inherited 'default behaviours'. These are the ways that we instinctively act or react, and they tend to be revealed most clearly when we are tired or under pressure. Sometimes our default behaviours are good and life-giving. But sometimes they are destructive and lead to the breakdown of family life and personal health, not only for the leader but also for those with whom they are working.

We should not confuse working long hours with effectiveness. The reality may be that the leader has no clear sense of what it is that they should be doing and what they should expect others in the organization to do. Far from being a good leader, they may be so arrogant that they think no one is as capable at doing the job as they are. They may be building an organization that is so dependent upon them that it may not survive when they leave or retire.

The usual response to 'I am constantly overtired' and 'I am only just coping' is to think that if I can get to the next weekend or holiday I will have time to recover. But that may be masking the underlying problem. The only way that the situation will change is if we examine our default behaviours and take responsibility for changing them.

One of the signs that there is something unhealthy in an organization is when people are constantly tired. There are, of course, periods in any organization when there are stresses or strains, when the unexpected has occurred and employees or volunteers have to work extra hours. But if tiredness is the norm, then there may be an organizational or personnel problem which needs addressing. For example:

- It may be that we are driven. The good side of this drivenness is that it has given us the energy and passion to build up an organization. But there can be a dark side to being driven which can eventually self-destruct or destroy others.
- It may be that the structures and resources of the organization have not changed as it has grown. We need to restructure it.
- It may be that we are not really willing or able to delegate properly.

Some people find their worth in demonstrating that they are able to work unbelievably long hours. But what is so admirable about having a large work capacity? Would it not be more worthwhile if we concentrated on improving the results of our work rather than the fact that we have to spend most of our lives in the office or on the factory floor? Why cannot we work in such a way that we can have proper time off and take all our holidays?

The first thing is to recognize our default behaviours and to be clear if they are destructive. We need to take responsibility for them. This is my problem, not the problem of the organization or the environment. As long as we go on blaming someone else we are in victim mode. This is something, as we will see in chapter 19, that can happen to whole organizations, usually to their long-term detriment.

At this point, someone usually says, 'Well, that is all very well. But clearly you do not understand the context in which I work – which is quite different.' If we claim that someone does not understand our organization, and there is no option except to work unreasonably long hours, then that in itself is part of our problem of perception. We are independent human beings with free will. We need to grow up and take responsibility.

Presuming that we have competent colleagues, then the reasons why we do not delegate are likely to be because of our desire for power or a lack of trust. Real delegation involves giving power away to others. However, if it is going to work we have to be clear about what we are asking the other person to do. Delegation is not the same as abdication.

Delegation is not saying 'Why don't you take on this portfolio?' without any parameters. The early stages of delegating something take a great deal of time and energy. Does the person know what is expected of them? What are they being asked to deliver? Do they know the scope of authority that we are giving to them? Do they know the limits of what they are being commissioned to do? The opposite problem is when we tell someone that we have delegated responsibility to them and then we keep checking up, thereby demonstrating that we are not sure if they are up to the job or that we do not think we can trust them.

For reflection

- What are your default ways of coping?
- If you find that you are constantly tired, what is the cause of it and what are you going to do about it?
- Reflect on how you delegate. Are your colleagues clear about what is expected? Do you trust them to get on with it?
- Do you bring others into your plans at an early stage? How willing are you to change your mind after listening to others?

7

Know how to reflect

George had built up a charity in his spare time and spare bedroom. At first he had done everything himself from answering emails, to fundraising and running the projects. Gradually he established an experienced team of colleagues. The charity was renowned for its effectiveness and dynamism. There was a culture of busyness.

In the early days George had not had time or resources to be able to take time out for reflection. However, as the charity grew he realized that he needed a day away from the office every month. He did not take his mobile phone or laptop. In addition, once a quarter, he took his senior team away for reflection. They did not have an agenda, only time for in-depth discussion on any subject that the team felt was important.

Many of the volunteers could not understand why the senior team needed to go off so regularly with no obvious immediate benefit. George believes that these days for reflection are the main reason for the success of the charity which still continues to grow.

Reflection sounds as if it is a very passive type of activity. Yet the opposite is true. The greatest sea changes that have come about in human history have been rooted in reflection, whether it was Archimedes' 'eureka moment' as he got into the bath, Copernicus's realization that the earth revolved around the sun or Darwin's breathtaking insights into evolution. The reality is that reflection is a difficult and demanding activity.

It stimulates action and promotes change. If you want a quiet and easy life do not develop the habit of reflection.

There is no simple method or technique of reflecting that will suit everyone. Each leader has to work out how to create the space and the means to reflect. Nevertheless, there are a number of underlying principles which may be helpful.

First, many individuals find it helpful to record their impressions, thoughts and reflections systematically. This is especially important if we have recently joined the organization from outside.

- What is strange or novel in this organization that surprises me?
- What are the values that are being espoused?
- What do people treat as significant or valuable?
- What are the things that I had expected to see or hear, but do not?

We only have a few weeks before we go native and adopt all the self-perpetuating myths that each organization nurtures to understand itself. However, if we are new we will probably see things with more clarity than those who are already part of the organization. These are some of the vital insights that we can bring and will help us formulate questions about the future.

It can be helpful to keep notes of the salient points that are being made and the names of those who are making them. This will provide us with a sense of history and continuity. A key task for the leader is to be able to describe and articulate the journey that the organization has made and where it is going.

Second, we need to recognize that one of the times when reflection is most needed is when everything seems to be going well. This sounds counter-intuitive. Surely we need to reflect most when we are facing crises or problems? But when there is a problem we know we have to think harder about how to respond to the difficulties. We are then more likely to consult others since we are worried.

Most organizations lose their way when there is just enough to do and just enough profit to keep everyone happy. Therefore, establishing a regular pattern for reflection is important. Some people can turn off from pressing matters and reflect quickly in the space of a few minutes. Most of us need more time. This is why we need free slots in the diary and a place where there is no distraction.

Third, in preparation for these times of reflection we need to assemble all the data and information that we think will be useful. It may mean taking financial trends and future planning documents with us. It may be helpful to listen to key individuals in different parts of the organization beforehand. We may want to find time to talk to those in the organization that we do not normally consult to see how they think things are going and if there are particular issues that need addressing. Some of those who work at the grass roots level of the organization see issues with a clarity that can be helpful.

Fourth, we need to ask questions. Being curious is a key prerequisite for reflection. It is helpful to ask open ended questions – the sort of questions that do not give away the answers that we would like to hear. Instead we have to allow people to articulate what they think in their own words. Are the explanations that others are giving us correct? How do we know that this is true? Are our assumptions right? Are we missing anything? What is it that we have not thought about yet?

Fifth, seek out those in the organization who are gifted in reflecting. There are some people who have a natural ability both to think and to be able to articulate their views. Nurture this gift in them; affirm them when they have a significant insight; and tell others about their contribution. This will encourage a culture of reflection in the organization.

Sixth, practise the habit regularly. Reflection is hard work, but it gets easier the more we do it. Some individuals in the organization will want us to be hands-on and involve ourselves mainly with operational matters. Attend to the operational when necessary. But we must not give in to our more activist colleagues and always react to what they are asking for. Our task is to be proactive in the way we reflect, working for the long-term thriving of the organization.

For reflection

- To what extent do you reflect on a regular basis?
- How can you do this more effectively and systematically?
- Why not block out time in the diary to ensure that you are reflecting adequately and regularly?

PART TWO

Understand others

Knowing yourself and understanding others are two complementary activities. Knowing yourself is important, but in isolation can lead to a preoccupation with being inward-looking. The counter-balance to an overemphasis on self-reflection is to focus on understanding others equally well.

Understanding the people we spend time with can provide a deep source of interest and joy. As we are allowed to enter the lives of others we are more able to encourage them, as well as find ourselves renewed and uplifted.

This section focuses on the importance of understanding others, nurturing the best in others, building common purpose, listening well and using feedback thoughtfully. It also addresses the importance of keeping an open mind and the learning that can come out of a crisis.

We hope that this section will reinforce the value you attach to understanding others. It is as we stand in the shoes of others and understand more of their hopes and fears that the quality of our reflection grows.

8

The importance of understanding others

Jill was asked to lead the organization without much warning. She was inexperienced and unsure how to deal with people. She was aware that Barry was causing ructions and having rows with colleagues. He was known for being aggressive, so Jill did not relish a confrontation. She hoped the problem would go away so she would not have to deal with it.

After one incident Jill asked to see Barry. She decided not to tell him off but to adopt a different approach. When Barry arrived he looked defensive and ready for an argument, presuming that she might want to sack him. 'I am really puzzled,' she told him. 'My take on you is that you are a highly gifted person and for some reason you are not contributing in a way that you could. We need your energy and skills if we are going to succeed. Tell me how you see the problem between you and your colleagues in your department.'

He was taken aback at her approach. He did moan about some of his colleagues but soon admitted that he knew he had got himself into a corner with his colleagues and that he was not playing his part. He said he wanted to change his approach and be a contributing member of the team.

The starting point was that Barry experienced Jill as being 'on his side'. He knew that she believed in him and his abilities. He heard her say that she presumed he was positive and well-intentioned. Barry knew that Jill assumed he would want to do something to improve his working relationships. Together they identified three things that he was going to do differently. Relationships in the team improved and their effectiveness increased. Within two years he became the team leader.

The most valuable asset in any organization is the people, whether employees or volunteers. An organization is more likely to thrive if they

- know they are valued for who they are
- are clear about what is expected of them
- consider that they are involved in something that is worthwhile
- are a valued member of a team
- know they have helped develop the corporate vision
- are fairly treated.

The endemic materialism of the Western world colours much of our thinking and acting. The unrelenting emphasis on financial reward sends out the subliminal message that the only sensible reason for working is to earn as much money as possible. This is one of the reasons why the media is so obsessed with different levels of pay. Of course, this is easy to say if we are not in the lower income bracket, when the promise of a little more money is very attractive and can still motivate a person to work longer hours.

But if the main reason for working is to receive the largest wages possible, why do so many millions of people choose occupations where the benefits are not primarily pecuniary? Why do others want to work long beyond retirement age, even when they have an adequate pension? Why are volunteers willing to undertake training and to commit to regular hours of work with charities? Is it not because work, whether paid or voluntary, can be a fulfilling activity in itself? It can be a profoundly satisfying thing, making us feel we have a role, providing the stimulation of colleagues and giving an outlet for our creativity.

For most individuals monetary rewards only motivate up to a certain point. Increasing numbers of people in high income occupations opt to work fewer hours for less money. The offer of an even larger bonus will not entice them to work longer or to take more hassle. Sometimes they use their additional free time to undertake voluntary work. This is because most of us want to feel that we are valued for who we are, not just for our skills, the contribution we make or the business that we can attract.

If a leader is always talking about money, they are likely to create an organization which sees itself mainly in monetary terms (Who earns the most? Who has the largest bonuses?). It will tend to attract people for whom the main motivation is earning more and more money. It will send out a message that the work itself has little intrinsic worth which is why ever larger rewards have to be offered to motivate the staff. It also assumes, in a subtle and largely unarticulated way, that customers are only useful for the financial contribution that they make. Most customers are not interested in the levels of staff pay, but are concerned about the quality and consistency of the product or service.

Conversely, leaders can be motivated by other values, such as those we discussed in chapter 2: 'I'm proud that these products are significantly enhancing the lives of our customers', 'We make first-class lawnmowers', 'As a company we are making a significant contribution to the local community', or 'We have changed our production techniques so that we are improving the environment'. If such values have a high profile in the corporate psyche of the organization, they will become increasingly important to the staff. Consequently they are likely to be less interested in what they can take out of the business and more committed to the difference that they are making. When someone goes into Marks and Spencer to buy a jersey, they are not motivated by wanting to increase the profitability of the company. They are looking for a product they like and for staff to give them the assistance that they need. Good care is attractive to customers. It builds up the company's reputation and helps it to thrive.

For reflection

- Reflect on your colleagues, their abilities, positive aspects and values. What motivates them?
- How can you build on this?
- How clearly, or not, do the motivations of your colleagues mirror your own, or are they very different? What can you learn from this?

9

The importance of nurturing the best in others

In one of the churches in Hertfordshire, there are some out-standing medieval corbels. These carved faces have been peering down from the ceiling on the worshippers for several hundred years. They are mounted so high up that it is difficult to see the details without a pair of binoculars. Each one of the faces has been skilfully carved and is unique.

When scaffolding was erected so repairs could be under-taken, it provided an opportunity to climb up and take a close look. People were amazed to find that on the reverse side of each head, facing the wall and not visible from any-where else, were also carved faces. Each one was carefully chiselled, and each one was different. The craftsmen had taken such delight in their work and felt it mattered so much, that they carved the reverse sides which would be seen by no one except God, and some curious people precariously balancing on scaffolding several hundred years later.

A good reputation is built on excellence. We can all think of organizations that are known for their first-class products and outstanding service. When there is a difficulty we are confident that they will listen to our concerns and do their best to rectify the problem quickly and efficiently. If you ask employees and volunteers no one ever says they want to work for a mediocre organization. They would all prefer to be part of something which is known for its good service or excellent products. We enjoy the kudos of contributing to something that has a high reputation.

Excellence is not just what we do but is an attitude. It comes from the way that we view our work and how we do it. Excellence attracts excellence, it inspires excellence. However, it is not the same as the neurotic or driven perfectionism of a leader who loses sight of what the organization is trying to achieve. A work colleague tells the story of one leader he met who insisted that staff spend hours colour coding receipts which made absolutely no difference to the service that they offered to their customers.

But why is it that some organizations are renowned for their excellence and others are generally considered to be poor? Where does excellence come from? Excellence originates from the leader. If the leader does not exemplify and practise it then standards will never be raised and people will be happy to put up with second best. Excellence has to be seen and be experienced at every level and in every activity of the organization. We are not going to provide a first-class service if the leader is regularly heard to say, 'I know it's a bit shoddy, but we are busy and it will just have to do.' We will never get a reputation for excellence if the car park is filthy or the receptionist inattentive. Excellence has to be the way that everything is done, from the smallest detail to the most important strategic decisions.

It is no good for the leader to talk about excellence if they do not demonstrate it. As in every area of life, the most basic factor that influences the way people act is the example of those in leadership roles. We tend to copy what we see and what we admire.

Having demonstrated excellence, the leader needs to make it one of the core values that they want and they expect of others. Organizations will only rise to the levels of the leader's expectations, but they never go higher. At this point the usual complaint is that we could provide excellence if we were able to charge more or if we have additional resources. Underlying this is the notion that if people do not pay much for goods or services then they should not expect much. But where does the notion that quality products or outstanding service and excellence have to be mutually exclusive? Why can we not provide basic services or low value products yet do so with the highest standards possible? Why can we not build a reputation of doing things superbly well?

The vast majority of individuals are willing to work hard and want to do a competent job. However, there are many reasons why people do not give of their best:

- They have spent years working in an environment where poor standards and low achievement are tolerated uncritically.
- We have already decided that they are not up to the job. The subliminal message we send is that we do not think they can rise to what is expected. If we really believe in people and invest in them they are more likely to meet the challenge.
- We do not expect enough of them. Over time people can change and standards can rise. We need to articulate our expectations consistently and find ways to celebrate the contribution of those in the organization who demonstrate excellence. If we do not believe that individuals can reach the highest levels of their ability then it is unlikely that many of them will do so. This includes everything from the kind of work that we ask people to perform, to the level of initiative that we expect them to demonstrate, to the degree of trust that we place in people. The end goal of all this is to have employees or volunteers who are proud to be part of the organization.

For reflection

- What are the ways in which I can draw out the best in others?
- To what extent do you personally exemplify excellence in your work and organization?

- How do you allow new volunteers or employees space to learn a task or to offer a service, while maintaining excellence?
- How are you helping others to rise to the challenge of 'excellence in all things'?

The importance of building common purpose

When the leadership team decided that the diocese needed a strategy, a small group of lay and ordained people were appointed and tasked with the work. After many meetings they presented a document with four main aims. Maureen was asked to implement this strategy across 450 churches and church schools. But how do you inspire, persuade and cajole large numbers of employees and volunteers in hundreds of different places to adopt a strategy which they have neither heard of or even particularly want?

Looking back, it is clear that the diocesan leadership should have begun the process by bringing a number of groups together to create the strategy. It would have been costly to hold a series of meetings, each with around a hundred people attending. But at the end of the process all the participants would have known why they needed a strategy, what were the key issues, the challenges and opportunities they were facing, and how they were going to go about it. Ironically, it turned out to be much more work for Maureen to visit all the churches and schools to explain what had already been decided and to persuade them to participate, than to have involved others in the first instance.

Organizations are like organisms. They are living entities and as such they are always changing and evolving. In larger organizations people are joining and leaving all the time. Everyone who joins will come with assumptions and expectations. They will have a set of values which may or may not be the values that you as leader think are important (such as excellence). They will also bring a range of ideas about the business or charity that they are joining, such as how the organization should be structured and how it should develop.

A leader should never assume that new employees or volunteers share their understanding of what the business is about. It is the task of the leader to ensure that everyone coming into the organization is inducted into its values and aims. It is not uncommon for organizations to lose direction because someone has joined who does not understand their core activity. With huge enthusiasm about an initiative or a development that worked well in their previous place of work, they have distracted the organization from its fundamental activity. They have lost focus.

There is a delicate balance here. As we observed in Chapter 7, one of the valuable gifts that a new person brings to an organization is their first impressions and insights. The leader needs to ensure that there are processes whereby their fresh perspectives can be articulated, debated and then integrated, as appropriate, into the core activity. There is, therefore, a vital task for leaders to be clear about their values and perspectives. These need to be spelt out clearly and regularly.

This process of communication is a complex one. The simplest things to communicate are what we are going to do ('We are moving offices', or 'We are launching a new service'). We need time to think about the implications that the decision will have for us, but we understand immediately what is being planned. The most complicated things to communicate or change are values ('We are going to improve the way we treat our volunteers', or 'We want to place a far higher emphasis on honesty'), because these have to be embodied in different ways of seeing things on a day-to-day basis.

Many leaders think that communication has happened because they have said something publicly or because they have put a notice up on the board. However, communication has not happened just because something has been said. It has only occurred when someone has heard and understood, in the sense of receiving the message and taking it on board. There is then a further step when what has been communicated is acted upon. One writer suggests that the way to improve communication is through 'multiple channels, multiple times'. How do you say the same thing over and over again, using all the means at your disposal?

A good way to communicate and to build common purpose is to bring together as many people as possible from across the whole organization and allow them to create the future plans. To do this the leader needs to set the context of the organization and to remind them of the 'givens'. When people are allowed to work away at common solutions and understand the reasons why we have come to such a decision, they are much more likely to want to implement them. Such a process is not a one-off event, but needs to be built into the life of the organization on a regular basis.

For reflection

- What are you doing to ensure that everyone in the organization has the same shared aims which contribute to what we are trying to achieve?
- How can you receive the insights from people new to the organization which may help you?
- How can you keep building a stronger, corporate sense of common purpose?

The importance of listening

Zoe knew the importance of asking the right questions in her role as senior nurse. When in charge of her ward, she would discreetly play back summary points to her colleagues at handover meetings with the result that they knew that their views had been heard and taken on board. Zoe demonstrated her leadership not only through the perceptive questions she asked, but in the way she asked them. She listened not only to the words, but to the emotions behind the words. She could sense when there was delight, anguish or pain. She could feel when heart and head were saying different things. Zoe also knew from the tone of voice whether there was consistency between the intellectual and the emotional, or if someone was unhappy about the expectations placed upon them.

Zoe drew on what she heard and saw in the way she led the ward. She knew instinctively that good listening meant leaving space and not rushing in to fill a silence in a conversation. Her respect for her colleagues, and the quality of her listening enabled the nursing staff to grow in confidence and make better decisions on priorities.

The best leaders are good listeners. Listening and leading are two sides of the same coin. A parish was waiting for its newly appointed vicar to arrive. Some people expected him to tell them his vision for the future. Others hoped that the new vicar would listen and learn first, and build a shared vision for the future. This latter group valued collaborative leadership where listening, learning and leading came in that order. In the event the vicar resisted calls from those who wanted an instant vision, and instead pursued a process of consultation with all the members of the church following an intensive period of listening. The vicar was conscious that while some clamoured for his attention, other less strident voices had just as important things to contribute. Both groups needed to be listened to, but the second group had actively to be drawn out to ensure their full participation.

Listening is about being open to the insights of people from different backgrounds and cultures. Some individuals will be articulate and others more reticent or economical in the words they use. Listening may involve shutting up certain people as diplomatically as possible once they have made their point lest they dominate a meeting, and enabling others who are less forthright to contribute. We may have to invite an individual by name to express their views. On key matters going round the table, asking people in turn to contribute, can ensure an equal voice from everyone.

Often good listening only happens when everyone has had ample time to reflect. When new information is presented or someone has opened up a fresh angle in a meeting, some people immediately know what they think and jump into the debate. But others need to mull over the implications of what they have heard. A judiciously chosen time for a coffee break is not just about satisfying thirst. It is about creating an opportunity for reflection which will promote a greater degree of consensus. When major decisions need to be taken, it is best to hold an initial meeting to review options and evaluate the information available. We can then allow a period for reflection before a second meeting when the decision is made.

Listening is about being aware of what is said and what is not being said. It is always worth reflecting on what comments are not being made. A debate might have moved on so points have become accepted and are no longer in contention. Points may not be made because they have become accepted or because they are in the 'too difficult' category. Discerning the difference is part of the skill of a reflective leader.

It is often worth summarizing where a discussion has reached and checking out with participants that they are content with the progress. Being conscious of whether or not the more silent people have spoken can lead to asking them directly if they have anything they would like to add.

Sometimes topics are not raised because they are politically or emotionally too difficult. Spotting such matters is crucial to understanding the dynamics in a meeting. It may not be the time and place to confront such issues, but the listening leader is aware of what is happening and will reflect on the implications.

Listening to someone who is inscrutable in their facial expressions can be unnerving. We rely on body signals to reinforce the words we hear. If someone looks cheerful our natural tendency is to do the same. If someone is scowling we tend to become more serious and might even scowl back. When listening to someone who is inscrutable there is an even greater need to check out our understanding with them. Perhaps the most difficult individuals to read are those where there is a discrepancy between words and body language. For the person who always appears jokey, the serious message may get lost because their manner continues to be light-hearted. Being conscious of cultural differences in the way individuals listen can bring valuable insights.

Reflecting on why someone is saying what they are saying and behaving in the way they are, is an essential part of listening. Good listening is about triangulating the different sorts of data that we are hearing, seeing and feeling. The leader's credibility will always rise when they are able to acknowledge that they have listened well and have acted upon what they have heard.

Listening is a continuous process and not a task that is ever fully completed. It is dangerous to presume we know what someone thinks or how they are going to vote on an issue. Real listening also presupposes that we will be willing to change our mind if the new information we hear warrants it.

We should always be ready for the 'I had not thought of that point' moment. The more we demonstrate that we are listening, the more we encourage people to modify their perspective in the light of fresh information and insights.

It is important that leaders understand what others both inside and outside the organization are saying about them and the organization. But dwelling too much on criticisms can be self-destructive. We need to take them on board without being crushed by them. Good listening will inevitably include hearing criticism. Some criticism will be unfounded but other comments may be justified. Such criticism can help us refine what we think and how to communicate it to others.

For reflection

- In what ways have you listened recently? What new understanding did you pick up?
- How well do you integrate what you hear and see when talking with different individuals?
- How best might you enhance your listening capabilities as a leader?
- What steps might you take to seek the views of the less-well heard?

12

The importance of feedback

Jane's company was struggling to survive in a difficult market. She became increasingly convinced that one of the main problems was the defensive attitude of her staff, especially two of her colleagues who were unwilling to take criticism or suggestions. Jane decided to set up a system of feedback. When she first broached the subject it was met with hostility, so much so that she was not sure it was going to be worth pushing the idea through.

After much thought, Jane realized the only way forward was to invite people in the company to give feedback on her leadership. She asked a former colleague, who had recently retired, to do this. Comments were to be made anonymously through the advisor. At first Jane decided that she wanted the feedback to be confidential, but after three months she summoned up the courage to make it public. Most of the feedback related to her leadership style and offered ideas about how she could lead more effectively. Jane tried to implement the ideas from the feedback and ensured that others in the organization knew what she was doing.

Six months later Jane suggested that everyone in the organization ought to receive feedback through a formal process. This time the idea was adopted with minimal dissent. People were convinced that feedback mattered and that it could make a difference. If Jane could benefit from it, so could they.

A fundamental aspect of reflection is giving and receiving feedback. How do we create a climate of sufficient trust where we can be honest with each other about what we are doing and the way we are doing it? How do we make it the norm that everyone's opinion matters? How do we give permission for people to contribute ideas about the future of the organization?

As in every other area we have explored, it has to begin with the leader. If the leader believes that feedback is important then they must be ready to receive it themselves from others in the organization. Unless the leaders make themselves vulnerable by being open to affirmation and criticism, no one else will be willing to do it. The way that the leader receives feedback and acts upon it sets the tone for the process throughout the organization. If the leader is wise and secure enough in themselves to acknowledge that they have learnt things about how they come across and how they can improve their contribution to the organization, then others are more likely to react in the same way.

One of the reasons why some individuals dislike feedback is that they have experienced it as something manipulative (the first step in being dismissed or of a competency procedure) or as being bullied by self-opinionated leaders who see themselves as above criticism. Most people are pretty astute. They know when feedback is being requested simply as a prelude to being criticized.

A crucial aspect about giving and receiving feedback is how it is done. Unless there is some honesty and integrity everyone will know that it is little more than a psychological trick. Feedback needs to focus on the task at hand and on behaviour. It is not about a person's character or an attempt to guess their motivations.

Second, we need to draw on the insights of Transactional Analysis. This is where both parties relate to each other in 'adult mode' as opposed to 'child mode' ('I can't cope', or 'I don't want to take responsibility for this') or 'parent mode' (either 'You are hopeless', or 'Shall I do this for you?'). We must not collude but help our colleagues take responsibility to grasp opportunities and to deal with problems. Adult mode is where we work alongside someone as a colleague, neither solving the problem for them nor leaving them to deal with it alone.

In practical terms this involves asking questions not pronouncing judgements. It means having the time and the energy to have a real conversation where we move beyond platitudes and identify the root causes of problems. For example, 'This is my perception about how you handled that situation. It is, of course, just my take on it. How do you see it?' This treats people as adults. However, such feedback needs time and attention to reflect on the sorts of questions that we ask and the way we respond to the answers. When feedback is experienced as judgemental, when it impugns my motives and criticizes my character, it will be destructive and will foster a negative culture.

The third thing about feedback is the tone with which it is offered. Does the other person experience you as someone who is on their side? Do they know that you want them to succeed? Do they sense that you think they can rise to the challenge and meet it? When a person is treated as an adult, and their experience and ability is affirmed, they are more likely to have time and energy to concentrate on what they are being asked to do.

For reflection

- Are you inviting feedback, and responding to it, in a way that encourages others to do the same?
- In what areas and to whom do you need to offer feedback?
- What are the best contexts in which to do this so it is received positively?

13

The importance of keeping an open mind

Robert was excited by his appointment as head of a large regional organization, following the retirement of a successful and widely respected manager. During a handover period, his predecessor alerted him to the fact that some of the senior staff were slow, unadventurous and difficult to work with. This advice, though kindly meant, had the unfortunate effect of colouring Robert's view of colleagues and he found it difficult to view senior staff other than through the spectacles of his predecessor.

It came as a pleasant surprise, therefore, when Robert was presented with some high quality pieces of work. He took a risk and, contrary to the advice of his predecessor, removed some of the constraints under which staff members were operating. Almost immediately he sensed an injection of new energy around the place. He realized that his initial judgements had been wrong. He began to talk with senior colleagues about why they had acquired a reputation for being unco-operative and cautious, and he realized that the situation he had inherited was not as straightforward as his predecessor had wanted him to believe.

After a while Robert came to admire his colleagues for their resilience in coping with difficulties. He apologized to them for his initial sceptical attitude, and expressed his appreciation of their skills and mutual support. A year into the post, Robert found himself heading a united team which was admired for being informed and adventurous. Robert had released new energy in the organization. His one regret was that he had allowed his predecessor to colour his judgements.

We carry both the benefit and the burden of our previous experiences. This means that we bring insights to situations, as well as preconceptions. Distinguishing between a valuable insight which has been honed by experience and a prejudice is not always straightforward. When we confront a problem, it can be helpful to write down what we regard as our personal predilections and jot down five perspectives we would normally have of such an issue. We may know instinctively whether a preference is in reality more akin to a prejudice. Sometimes it is only through discussing and triangulating our views with others that we begin to see the extent to which a personal preference is an honest starting assumption or merely a prejudice in disguise which blurs our objectivity.

This is not easy territory to navigate. One person's conviction about the best way forward might be another person's prejudice. It is vital, therefore, to start from a position which treasures human dignity and independence. If we write off a particular group of individuals, we are at risk of letting prejudice blind us to their qualities and potential contribution.

A good leader believes that a person can learn from experience and be transformed, while accepting that for a small number of individuals change will be limited, if not impossible. For example, an individual who is unwilling or unable to give a lead to their staff cannot be allowed to continue in post for the long term. Someone who refuses to modify their behaviour and continues to be disruptive needs to be asked to move on for the sake of everyone else, however painful this might be. The hope is that they will be able to change after the shock of an exit, if they are not willing to change within the job itself.

There is always a risk that we make snap decisions about what a person is capable of or what they can contribute to the organization. Being honest with ourselves when we put someone in a box can be a key starting point. When we see the prospect of someone changing or spot an openness to change, we need to invest more fully in that person's future.

Heather never thought that Esther would be able to chair a meeting well and so had written off the possibility of asking Esther to deputize for her. When Heather was ill, there was no option other than Esther chairing the meeting. When she returned to work Heather heard reports about Esther's superb chairing and commented publicly about how well she had done. Heather now decided she needed to give Esther more space to grow. She encouraged her to chair future meetings. Esther grew hugely in confidence once she knew that Heather was willing to support her and give her new opportunities.

Being ready to be surprised creates an open and healthy attitude of mind. We are always on the look-out for how individuals and situations might change. We become more alert to potential opportunities. This can apply as much to ourselves as to others. If we are surprised about how we have reacted in a particular context, we need to pause and reflect on the experience. We may be able to learn something new about ourselves. Keeping an open mind is not about going into a situation ill-prepared. It is about standing back and asking, why was I not expecting this? In this way, we keep a freshness of mind and an openness of heart that means that we do not write off ourselves or others easily.

We will grow in effectiveness as leaders if we take time to reflect on those occasions when we have been pleasantly surprised or unexpectedly taken aback. These experiences can provide us with a wealth of insight. No situation is static. There will always be changes in attitudes and understanding to be observed. Confronting our own prejudices and ruthless self-examination are essential skills in the toolbox of a successful leader. It enables us to retain a healthy balance between maintaining a sense of direction and indulging curiosity, so that new information, perspectives and insights are welcomed rather than feared.

For reflection

- Think of a demanding situation you have encountered recently. What made it difficult? Are there any prejudices you brought to this situation which may have acted as a barrier to resolving it effectively?
- Have you recently been surprised by how someone reacted in a difficult situation? What did you learn?
- How can you ensure that you do not miss an important insight about a situation when you bring your particular perspective or prejudice?

14

The importance of a good crisis

The charity had been founded in 1963 to support people living with a degenerative disease. It had built up a large group of volunteers across the south of England. Tensions had grown between one of the trustees and the chief executive. The trustee resigned and left, setting up a rival charity. He took the finance director with him, along with some of the volunteers.

The loss of so many supporters was a serious blow and threatened the future of the charity. It seemed inevitable that some of the most experienced staff would have to be made redundant. An emergency meeting was called which was open to everyone who had any link with the charity, including some of the people living with the disease. It was a tough meeting. Quite a few of the supporters had felt increasingly alienated from the direction that the charity had been going in. There was a consensus that communication had been poor. They felt they were being taken for granted. A couple of doctors were critical that the charity was out of touch with the latest research which should have affected the way the services were being offered.

Angela, the new chairwoman of the trustees, was strong and wise enough to let everyone have their say, despite the protestations of the chief executive who felt threatened. Angela ensured that all the points that were made were recorded and she stressed that they would be reflected upon carefully. She spelt out the seriousness of the situation and asked the supporters to identify other people who might be able to help.

> The result was that the charity refocused its work, recruited a newer and younger group of volunteers and has now grown. The events that could have brought the organization down became the means of its growth.

Most of us think that crises are inevitably bad things. We worry about the future ('What will happen if we go bankrupt?' 'How will we cope if all the volunteers resign?') and what is going to happen to me ('Will I lose my job?'). At worse we may lose sleep and our health may suffer.

Of course, there are some crises which are so serious that they destroy or damage an organization for years. In 1991 Gerald Ratner's ill-advised comments about the quality of his company's products had a devastating effect on their sales from which his company never recovered. The Buncefield explosion at an oil storage terminal in 2005 created the largest conflagration in the UK for 30 years. Several years on, the site is still closed. A dishonest treasurer can damage trust in a church or charity for decades.

Leaders have a number of basic responsibilities when it comes to crises that no one else can shoulder. The first one is that they need to think long and hard about the threats that face the organization, so they can be pre-empted at the earliest opportunity. Of course, some crises by their very nature cannot be foreseen. However, it is possible for leaders to put time aside on a regular basis to think about the way that they might approach certain sorts of crises should they occur.

The second responsibility is that leaders should have the time and energy to respond to a crisis when it occurs. It is no good if we are so exhausted in dealing with day to day management issues that we have no resources when things start going wrong. When we are tired and harassed we may not make wise decisions. We need to have time in the diary and reserves of energy available for times of crisis. Many people felt that the response of BP to the oil leaks in the Gulf of Mexico in 2010 could have been handled better if the leadership team had responded more quickly and sensitively.

Third, leaders need to think about the steps they are going to take when confronted with a crisis. For example, they may have thought through who in the organization would need to be brought together to respond to what is unfolding. This is not dissimilar to the concept of the War Cabinet which included politicians from the opposition, where problems could be discussed and examined from every angle. Such a team may include heads of departments, communications officers, personnel and legal advisors.

One of the most difficult periods for a leader to use effectively is when a company or a charity is going just well enough to keep everyone quiet. It is in times such as these that a minor crisis, with wise and steady leadership, can become a means of growth and new direction. A crisis can be used to get rid of old, destructive divisions and to destroy unhelpful power bases. A common enemy or threat can help get things back into perspective. It can provide a reason to call everyone together and agree to co-operate to survive the pressing challenges. Once the immediate challenge is resolved it is important not to allow individuals to lapse back into their old ways of working.

Fourth, it is helpful to have identified which of your colleagues work well under pressure when things are difficult. People who can keep a cool head when others are panicking are invaluable and need to be brought into the discussions at the earliest opportunity.

For reflection

- What are the sorts of crises that your organization might face?
- Have you decided on the way that you would approach them?
- Who would you need to consult and bring with you?

PART THREE

Create a flourishing team

A leader can never operate effectively in isolation. The good leader will always work with a team around them, motivating, encouraging and stimulating a wide group of people so that they all give of their best.

Such a team will be more than the sum of its parts. As it works collaboratively, the team will have the energy, resolve and creativity which the individuals acting singly would never have been able to generate.

This section discusses how to create a positive team. How do we find space to reflect together? How can we develop a coaching culture and an environment where dissenting voices are heard? It addresses the importance of engendering a positive culture, with the capacity to make decisions. The section concludes with the importance of celebration.

Perhaps the most important responsibility for any leader is to grow a team where individuals are engaged and where they learn from each other. Members of a flourishing team value and celebrate each other's perspectives. They are not daunted by conflict, but see constructive debate as an opportunity to work towards creative, well-thought-through conclusions.

15

Create a positive team

Frank was a valued member of the leadership team in his organization. He and his colleagues thought it was by far the most effective team they had ever been part of. Years later they still keep in contact with each other and meet up regularly to celebrate and support each other.

Why was it such a memorable team? Its members were very different in their background and approach. The secret of their success lay in the fact that they accepted one another at quite a deep level and had learnt to trust one another's judgement. This is not to say that mistakes were not made from time to time. But these were talked through and never ridiculed. There was a strong sense of wanting each member of the team to do well.

They recognized the gifts and contributions each person brought to the table. Debate was invariably robust, but never destructive. They were committed to moving forward decisions effectively and to foster a common vision right across the organization. The fact that the senior leadership team was positive, energetic and creative created a ripple effect which meant that the same behaviours were legitimized, encouraged and recognized at every level of the organization.

Creating a positive team requires a set of agreed aims and a sense of shared endeavour. The senior leadership team in a government department was determined to ensure that the ministers would have confidence in a group of people who were capable and determined to lead an ambitious agenda set by the new government.

Relationships of trust were established quickly between officials and ministers. A vision was agreed between the secretary of state and the permanent secretary and then owned by the wider group of senior officials. Because the sense of direction was clear and a willingness to take a strong lead was evident, it was relatively straightforward for both the leadership team and individual members to be positive in their approach. They knew where they were going and had confidence in each other's contribution. Potential obstacles were overcome rather than throwing the team off course.

What motivated this team and others like it was not status or money. The team members wanted to make a difference. For some this came from a long-term commitment to the policy areas the department dealt with. For others it arose from a sense of public service. Some individuals held an explicit religious or philosophical belief in the importance of improving opportunities for individuals and communities.

The best of teams 'give their all'. They are committed to what they are doing and believe passionately that they can make a difference. But building trust is not easy. Misunderstandings have to be overcome and trust re-established. Poor communication has to be sorted out. The vagaries of our human nature, including our innate selfishness, means that maintaining trust is a costly business but one which yields rich dividends.

Petra was part of a governing body of a sixth form college for a number of years where the college was making a significant difference in the lives of young people. The college stretched the expectations of the students and enabled them to go on to demanding courses of higher education, having built their understanding on a positive foundation of learning at the college.

The role of the governing body as a leadership group was to bring their diverse backgrounds to help crystallize the ambition of the executive members. The positive attitude of the governing body enabled the principal and his senior leaders to be confident in the direction they were taking the college. Having trust in the senior staff and setting them free to do their work well, was an important contributory factor to the success of the college.

Creating a positive team requires us to think clearly about what is motivating our colleagues. How can we set them free from what holds them back? How can we hold a team together and at the same time liberate its members to make an energetic, innovative and profound contribution to the success of the organization?

Mutual understanding can be enhanced by the use of personality profiles. Perhaps the best-known and most frequently used is the Myers Briggs Type Indicator. It can be a useful tool to help us understand each other's strengths and weaknesses. It provides insights about the different ways in which we respond to each other, to crises and challenges.

In successful teams the leader is invariably skilled at 'reading' colleagues, and understanding what motivates them so that they give of their best. One of the key tasks of leadership is to identify the contexts or the prompts which enable a person to thrive and be effective. The goal is to liberate people to make their contribution with confidence and flair, and so to orchestrate the interaction between the team members that the overall outcome is more than the sum of the parts.

The best teams, therefore, enable and stimulate individuals to be creative. They foster an ethos of shared endeavour. Team members form themselves into working partnerships of twos and threes which add to and never detract from the overall impact of the team. A good team will be built on a base of strong partnerships both within the team and with people external to the organization. They are founded on shared values, on trust based on experience, and the recognition of agreed outcomes.

Where a team is driven by status, perks or money, it is possible that tensions within it may cause friction and erode a sense of shared responsibility. If a team becomes unhealthily introspective and loses its positive drive, it may need to be dismantled and individuals moved to new responsibilities elsewhere in the organization. A team that struggles to find a common purpose probably needs to be disbanded sooner rather than later, and effort focused on building a fresh vision with a new team.

For reflection

- What are the characteristics of a team you have been part of that had a positive impact? What enabled that team to become a force for good?
- What are the characteristics of the leadership of a team where members are strongly motivated?
- How can you enable teams you are part of to be more positive?

16

Create space for reflection

Difficult issues always require careful analysis and rigorous objectivity. The pressure of day-to-day business on a leadership group, however, can be relentless. Sometimes it means that decisions have to be made quickly. What made the leadership group at a major hospital so effective was the creation of space for reflection. On a regular basis the senior team would move out of its formal decision-making role into a more informal context for reflection.

They would meet away from the hospital at a neutral venue and talk about issues from a longer-term perspective. Discussion was interspersed with a brisk walk or, on one occasion, a visit to an art gallery during a lunchtime. They used a variety of approaches to stimulate new energy and fresh perspectives. The desire to foster a more reflective quality enabled the group to stand back, identify trends clearly and understand longer-term opportunities. Creating space for reflection was no indulgence; it was central to the success of the team keeping 'ahead of the game'.

It is easy to think that success comes only through constant action. Some leaders fear reflection because it may give colleagues the opportunity to question the direction they are going in and whether they are meeting their objectives. However, a team that does not reflect will soon become exhausted. It can rush headlong into problems and find controversies that it had not realized existed exploding all over the place. It soon descends into turmoil. Such a team risks being unaware of what might hit it and can become oblivious to new opportunities. Like an excited group of youngsters in a fast car, they neither see the tight bends coming, nor have any sense of the dramatic landscapes they are passing or new vistas that are opening up before them.

The best advice for any team with a passion to get on with their work can be to take time to reflect and to reassess. At the very least, taking time out gives an opportunity to pause and allow a breathing space. At best, pausing for thought can lead to some re-evaluation and reshaping. Reflecting corporately as a team is an investment in leadership capital to sustain the future of an organization.

However fast the team is moving, there is always time to reflect. Even when there is a tight deadline with a contract needing to be signed tomorrow there can be the opportunity for both the sharing of information and perspective, and the opportunity for quiet reflection before a decision is made. The best of leaders going through turbulent times know that pressing the pause button in order to stand back quietly is an essential part of effective decision-making.

Reflection by a leadership team is not an optional extra, but a necessity. The types of approaches that can be used include:

- Periodic meetings in a different environment to consider the long-term agenda.
- The use of an external facilitator to help promote a different sort of discussion.
- Individuals sharing their perspectives about long-term opportunities and risks.
- A team coach observing discussions and feeding in a wider perspective.
- Members of the team doing different things together such as walking, being part of a sports team or looking at a creative piece of work which is different from the area they are currently involved in.

A half day or day out to think and reflect can easily be branded a waste of time. But many teams testify that such events have helped create new bonds between team members and become a turning point in the life of the organization. If such thinking time is going to be productive, it is essential to understand what stimulates optimal reflection. For some it will be talking issues through or envisaging future circumstances and outcomes. For others it is the stimulus that comes from hearing a fresh perspective from an outside speaker. Some value being in a small group to discuss different scenarios in confidence. Others need solitude to reflect by themselves before re-entering a team's deliberations. Catering for individual preferences is not easy, but in the long run the dividend is enormous in terms of a more profound analysis and sharper understanding.

Space for reflection is often linked to sharing a meal. Many religions stress the importance of eating together as a way of bonding as a group. The sense of communion is strengthened by eating and sharing in a reflective way. But this does not guarantee that we get all the answers right. Henri Nouwen, the Dutch theologian wrote, 'The art of living is to enjoy what we can see and not complain about what remains in the dark ... Let's rejoice in the little light we carry and not ask for the great beam that would take all the shadows away' (*Bread for the Journey*, Darton Longman and Todd, 1996, p. 16). Reflection enables us to discern the next step even if we are not clear about the next mile.

When a leadership team decides on the method of reflection that works best for them it gives an important signal to the rest of the organization. If a senior team does not make time for reflection, they should not be surprised when others feel inhibited from doing so. If they value time for reflection and can demonstrate that they have used that time well, then others will feel liberated to do the same. This is not about legitimizing excessive jaunts or wasting money. It is about affirming the value of reflective space.

For reflection

- How best have teams you have been part of created space for reflection?
- What types of reflection by teams do you observe have been most beneficial?
- How might teams you are part of create more space for reflection and how might they use that space well?

17

Create a coaching culture

Jennifer was part of the governing body of an educational institution where relations with the principal were strong, and relations with the vice principal were strained. The principal came to governing body meetings in a spirit of openness, sharing successes and issues, and wanting to hear views. At the meetings members felt able to ask questions, there were good quality exchanges with a sense of warm engagement and purposeful conversation in which no one was defensive or aggressive.

In contrast the vice principal was guarded. On some occasions he seemed to give limited information, appeared rather close-minded and never asked the governing body members for their views. As a result, they felt excluded and asked sharp rather than open-ended questions, and felt left out rather than embraced. The result was that the vice principal became even more defensive and the governing body members did not feel well served.

This contrast within one institution demonstrates how creating open, reflective discussion can enhance or, if it is not done, damage the quality of interaction. Encouraging a coaching culture in an organization is about building an openness to learn from each other and the ability to ask and answer open-ended questions well. One of the most important skills of any leader is to be able to ask perceptive questions in a way that elicits thoughtful responses that help crystallize next steps. It is not only the quality of the questions, it is the way in which they are asked.

There are moments when it is appropriate to ask incisive questions that put an individual on the defensive. When an interrogator is trying to put someone on the spot, the acute observation of body language as well as the words is important. But in many cases it is the open-ended question asked in a relaxed way which can be the more productive form of question. When someone is at ease they are more likely to give a full answer than when they have been put on the defensive.

If someone is always being questioned by other members of a team, it may be unsettling and unproductive. The individual can feel that they are a victim. The frequent reaction when questioned intensively is to place the responsibility or blame on someone else. When an investment broker is asked why an investment decision went wrong, the natural reaction is for the analyst to blame those who gave wrong information.

Open-ended questions might include:

- What opportunities may be opening up?
- What is your experience over the last few weeks?
- What might be the future options?
- With whom is it important to build an alliance?
- How best is the success of the team built upon?

An open-ended question cannot be answered by saying yes or no. It invites a response which explores future possibilities rather than repeating set answers.

Effective leadership is about creating a situation where individuals readily take responsibility for the decisions they have taken. Using open-ended questions rather than an accusatory style is more likely to lead to people saying why they took the decisions they did and means the truth is reached more quickly.

There will be times when the best form of leadership is giving unequivocal advice, but to use this approach all the time can be ultimately destructive. Good leaders learn to refine the questions they ask in such a way that individuals reach their own conclusion rather than the leader using the authority of their position to tell people what to do or to give them direct advice.

In a team that is working well, individual members will seek out colleagues to talk issues through and seek their perspective. Asking a colleague for help is not a sign of weakness. Rather it is a recognition that we do not know all the answers. A colleague who enables us to work through an issue may be valuable in helping us see the key considerations and clarify the next steps.

Creating a coaching culture is both about the quality of questions and about being curious and legitimizing curiosity. Where the instinctive response might be 'I think my colleague is wrong', a more constructive question might be, 'Why does my colleague think in that way?' The more curious we are about the perspectives that other people bring, the more we will understand them and be able to empathize with them.

Curiosity is not just something we want to encourage in a seven-year-old. It is a quality that keeps us fresh and engaged. It helps us understand where other people are coming from. Sometimes, particularly when new to an organization, curiosity can be inhibited by a fear that a question may appear stupid. Paradoxically having the confidence to appear stupid and ask a question or articulate a thought can raise a concern felt by others in the same room.

It is as we are curious and explore our curiosity that we reflect and see different perspectives. As you walk around a lake you see reflections of different hills or trees. Sometimes the reflection is still and perfect. On other occasions, it is partial and moving. As we encourage a questioning style and the use of curiosity within teams, we enable them to reflect both individually and together even more effectively.

For reflection

- Think about a situation you will face or a meeting you will attend. Jot down some open questions which you may be able to use.
- How might you be more curious in the way you understand where different people are coming from?
- How can you create a culture of coaching in your team?

18

Create a culture where dissenting voices can be heard

Simon was chair of the trustees of a charity that had a large property in London. While undertaking repair work, it became clear that there were serious problems with the back walls which would need considerable extra sums of money to be spent. The only way the charity could finance this was by taking out a large loan. After a lengthy debate the governing body voted to go ahead.

One member, Michael, dissented. He was an expert in finance and he did not think that the charity would be able to repay the loan. He felt so strongly that he resigned. Most of the trustees were sorry that he left, but after a long discussion they still went ahead with the decision.

Within a few months it became clear to all the trustees that they were wrong and that Michael had been right. The bank called in the loan. It was only because of some very quick and decisive action by the chairman (who was able to bring in a large grant from an outside body at short notice) that the charity did not go bankrupt. The trustees were forced to reflect: why had they not been willing or able to listen to the dissenting voice?

Making the best decisions in a situation can be a complex business. Some organizations have been destroyed by making a wrong or ill advised decision. One of the vital tasks for a leader is to ensure that we make as many good decisions as possible. Normally the best way to do this is through consultation and discussion, bringing around the table all those who understand the issues. However, consensus does not always lead to the right decision. As one writer of a piece of graffiti put it, 'Surely 100,000 lemmings can't all be wrong.'

The reasons why groups do not always make the best decisions are complex. Sometimes the leader may feel that a decision must be made even when all the data is not available. Pressures such as a potentially difficult annual general meeting or because a key person is going to be out of the country for a couple of weeks, should never force groups into making hasty decisions.

At other times poor decisions are made because those in leadership have got out of touch with some fundamental facts about the area they are working in or have failed to spot a long-term emerging trend. It is also possible for groups to get into a negative dynamic and talk themselves into a course of action that is not the best one. Irving Janis, reflecting on what some writers have called 'Groupthink', described this phenomenon as: 'A mode of thinking that people engage in when they are deeply involved in a cohesive in-group, when the members' strivings for unanimity override their motivation to realistically appraise alternative courses of action' (*Groupthink: Psychological Studies of Policy Decisions and Fiascoes*, Boston MA: Houghton-Mifflin, 1972, p. 9).

One of the commonly cited examples of Groupthink was President Kennedy's decision to invade the Bay of Pigs in Cuba in 1961, which in retrospect turned out to be a serious mistake. An expedition force of 1400 Americans was overwhelmed. Over 1200 surrendered and some died. Kennedy was later reported to have asked, 'How could I have been so stupid?' He called it 'a colossal mistake'. One of his principal advisors, Arthur Schlesinger, later said, 'In the months after the Bay of Pigs I bitterly reproached myself for having kept so silent during those crucial discussions in the cabinet room. I can only explain my failure to do more than raise a few timid questions by reporting that one's impulse to blow the whistle on this nonsense was simply undone by the circumstances of the discussion' (*Groupthink*, p. 39).

Groupthink is more likely to happen in the following conditions:

- when there is a leader with strong views
- where the leadership group has a strong sense of corporate identity and has an over-optimistic view of its abilities
- where stereotyping is used to characterize opponents or competitors
- where the organization feels pressurized, for example from the media or its supporters, to make a decision.

St Benedict gives guidance about making decisions in a monastic community. He says that the whole community should be summoned so that the abbot can take counsel, although he also notes, 'It is often to a younger brother that the Lord reveals the best course.' In other words, it may be the newest member of the organization who sometimes sees things with a clarity that the old timers have lost. It is here that we need to pay special attention to dissenting voices. We need to cultivate discernment.

There are some people who for a variety of reasons will always want to take a different view from the majority. But what about the times when someone who is well respected is not in agreement? The leader should not push for a quick consensus but allow time for the person who genuinely sees the position differently to express their views. By patient questioning we need to draw out and assess the reasons why someone is dissenting. It is here that some of the strongest leaders have an Achilles heel. The danger is that others may not want to voice their opinions: 'There's no point – he has already decided. He never changes his mind anyway. He always thinks he is right.'

Not only are leaders who never change their mind difficult to work with but they are probably not very good at their job. Much better is the leader who says, 'Provide me with a better solution or idea and I will be glad to adopt it.' This creates

a culture where the contribution of those with the best ideas
and insights are acknowledged and celebrated.

For reflection

- How do you encourage individuals with dissenting views
  to voice their opinions?
- How do you show that people with genuine insights, even
  if they go against the grain of much of the past, will be
  respected and valued?

19

Create a positive culture

It was an attractive looking church building which was home to a committed congregation of about 50 adults and a handful of children. Andrew, a church consultant, was asked by the vicar to help the leadership team plan for the future. He began by getting everyone to engage in a brainstorm, describing their strengths and weaknesses. They then went on to discuss the five most important priorities.

All was going well until they tried to turn these aspirations into plans. Whenever anything was suggested someone would say, 'We've tried that before – it didn't work then and it won't work now.' After a while Andrew realized that this small but committed group of people were in 'victim mode'. Although they said they wanted to move forward and look outwards to their community, they were much happier being dependent, where everything was someone else's fault and where they did not have to make any changes that may upset their cosy life.

Every leader has to face difficult challenges. Sometimes these come from within the organization or they may be things that hit us unexpectedly from outside. Frequently these involve colleagues, whether it is an unexpected illness or someone who is deemed to be under-performing. At such a point there is a danger of going into 'victim mode'. It is much easier to project all the problems onto someone else or some external event outside our control. We can then blame others or the situation for what is going wrong, rather than take the harder path, which is to confront the difficulties and decide how to respond to them.

There is probably not an organization in the world that does not suffer from victim syndrome. Think about your own work context. Is there someone who is considered not up to the job, or is not pulling their weight? The easy thing to do is to sit back and blame them. During coffee breaks the discussion revolves around how much better it would be if we could replace that person with someone who is more competent or co-operative.

It is worth recognizing that this is the case in virtually every organization. Even the most forward-looking and dynamic companies fall into this trap at times. Thinking that this is only a problem for your organization is itself an expression of being in victim mode.

There are times when someone is not up to the job and we have to decide what to do about it. They may have to leave the organization. But sometimes the person can do the job if they are given the right support. The problem may be because they had become the focus of our corporate frustrations within the organization.

The challenge of leadership is to work out how to get alongside this individual and find out if there are ways in which they can do their job better. Inevitably it takes time to listen to what really makes the person tick, but working with them may be the right solution for the organization rather than sacking them and finding a replacement which may take months and cost a great deal of money.

External events or circumstances can become an excuse for an organization feeling a victim. We can talk ourselves into believing that there is nothing we can do in the present climate. So we allow ourselves to remain in victim mode. Often underlying this is a sense that we are being controlled by forces outside our influence. If so, this is a world view which is hard to shift.

One of the differences between a poor leader and a good leader is how they respond to such events. A good leader does not spend large amounts of time hiding behind things that they cannot change. The secret is to identify the areas where there is a possibility of making a difference and concentrating on them. This involves thinking outside the box and spotting different ways of approaching problems or finding new areas to explore.

For example, John and Caroline Jones grow tomatoes commercially in Hertfordshire. In a very tough competitive market many other growers have gone out of business. John and Caroline have innovated continually over the years. In 2000 they installed combined heat and power units, so that they now run five micro turbines to produce their own electricity. The exhaust gasses are pumped into the greenhouse to increase the level of CO_2. Excess electricity is sold. In 2007 they built an anaerobic digestive system. This is designed with five cells so it can be run continually and never closes down. Spitalfields Market among others brings their vegetative waste for free to feed it. The methane gas that they produce now runs the generators. By diversifying and innovating they have kept ahead of the market.

Good leaders recognize that there are areas in which they can make a difference, an improvement or an efficiency, and they seize these opportunities with both hands. What began as a crisis has turned them into a more efficient business.

One of the most powerful tools for getting people out of victim mode is story. If someone else or another organization has been able to overcome a similar problem or break new ground at the same time that we are feeling defeated, then it tells us that positive things can be done. A good leader is always on the look out for living examples of individuals or groups who have innovated or developed a new service or product in parallel situations to their own.

For reflection

- Reflect on your areas of responsibility. Are there colleagues or departments who are in victim mode?
- Can you think of stories that would challenge this and provide an alternative narrative?

20

Creating the capacity to make decisions

Paul was outstanding at creating the right context for decisions to be made in the school of which he was head. He
enabled all the members of the senior staff team to have
their say. He was assiduous in ensuring the wider group
of teachers had the opportunity to input their views in
advance. In the meetings staff felt able to contribute, but
knew they needed to make their points concisely. Under
Paul's headship most decisions 'just happened'. He created the environment where a consensus was reached, with
those who had expressed a different view normally being
willing to go along with the majority perspective.

Paul generated an atmosphere among the senior staff of
the school that was both reflective and reassuring. At the
same time he was clear when decisions had to be made and
who had the responsibility to make them. As a consequence
individuals were more willing to reach agreement than if they
had been lectured or eye-balled into submission. It was only
in retrospect that participants fully acknowledged Paul's
skilfulness in steering the decision-making process. It was
part of the secret of Paul's success as head teacher.

Creating the capacity to make decisions is not just about
ensuring that other people provide the right information. It is
about enabling everyone with a stake in an issue to play their
part in the decision-making process. When it is known that

the leader makes all the decisions, other members of the team are liable to feel disenfranchised and, as a result, will be only partially committed to them. This will be evidenced in their lack of energy and drive to make a given decision a success.

Effective leaders do not foster an expectation that they need to make and implement all the decisions themselves. Instead they enable the team to reach a consensus as often as possible. They equip and authorize others to make decisions within their areas of responsibility. A wise leader will only take decisions in a limited number of areas where no one else can do it. Success is about enabling others to make good decisions.

Effective leaders reflect back to their team why some decisions have to be made rapidly and with minimal consultation. Often this is because of a tight timescale imposed by external factors. Without a shared set of values and an agreed protocol, this can undermine trust within an organization. Normally, a leader with foresight explains why certain decisions have to be made and enables full conversation, with the result that decisions are taken more slowly.

Unanimity is a wonderful goal, but it is not always achievable. Reaching a majority view in which others will acquiesce is often a more realistic aspiration. It is vital, therefore, to give space for those uneasy about a decision to talk through their reservations. It will help them let go of any resentment, move forward and support the majority view.

Observing how others create capacity within their organizations for effective decision-making is always an interesting exercise. People will often mirror the attitude of their seniors. Thus a leader who says, 'I am sure we can work this out', provides a sense of reassurance and shared endeavour which is likely to elicit a similar response from members of the team. Conversely, an aggressive leader is likely to elicit a negative reaction and end up with a depressed team of colleagues.

It can also be salutary to observe leaders trying to cajole others into submission. Such coaxing might include claims to more knowledge or experience, the use of charm, anger, or working through a selected sub-group of similarly minded people. There will be moments when it is right to assert particular knowledge or experience. It is always appropriate to use a warm and engaging approach. Occasionally controlled anger can be effective, but if overdone, will be self-defeating. Working through selected small groups has its place too. But this can create an 'in crowd', and unwittingly undermine and limit a sense of creativity and common purpose in the wider team. The litmus test will always be whether a person is building genuine shared ownership of decisions, or whether the agreement is only skin deep.

Leaders need to be especially wary if they take a decision which empowers only a few. A strong leader will have the confidence to widen the decision-making forum to include others with differing perspectives. We need to be alive to the motives of those who seek to protect their position of influence by preferring to keep decision-making within a restricted group they can control.

Expanding the capacity for decisions to be made well in an organization or group needs also to recognize the different ways individuals come at issues. Each person brings his or her own set of preferences and prejudices. It is important, therefore, to achieve a balance between clarity and conviction in the process. Clarity ensures that the information on which decisions are made is robust, and that the group is furnished with detailed analysis and a full appreciation of the views of different stakeholders. Conviction relates to a person's instinctive reaction. Conviction corresponds to a person's innate values or experiences.

Creating the capacity to make decisions is then about enabling both individuals and a team to be bold and courageous, not in a foolhardy way but in a way that weighs up both potential benefits and the risks. Making decisions is not about hiding the risks or downsides; it is about facing them head on and deciding honestly and thoughtfully what the right next steps are.

Sometimes emotional reactions to a decision can be ridiculed. But emotional reactions can provide valuable data. A sense of alarm might be an irrational fear, but it might alert us to be cautious or to seek further information. There is no fail-safe rule at this point. 'Trust your instinct' is the best maxim. A good decision is more likely to emerge and to enjoy support when care and courage are brought together. We need to think carefully about the effect of our decisions on the hopes and aspirations of others. We also need the courage to make the right decision even if it causes pain for others. Few decisions are painless, which is why care and courage have to sit alongside each other lest a leader becomes callous.

For reflection

- Who do you observe who creates the capacity for good decisions to be made? What can you learn from them?
- What are the psychological ploys you sometimes use to get people to agree with you? Are they legitimate?
- How might you use your intuitive reactions more effectively when reflecting on what is the best way forward on a particular decision?

21

Create a culture of celebration

Keith loved arranging celebrations. He would revel in telling stories about an individual's or a group's success. If there was ever an opportunity to stand up and say a few words of congratulation, he would be the first to do so. He was a master of telling stories that encapsulated how individuals had coped with difficulties and ensured that a good outcome was achieved.

Both staff and volunteers in the organization appreciated Keith's emphasis on celebration and thanking people. His words of personal praise and his strong message of recognition enabled them to glow inside and fully appreciate the contribution they had made. Sometimes they could feel a shade embarrassed, but the pluses of Keith's acknowledgement far outweighed any sense of 'what is he going to say next?' The tone of celebration that Keith set reinforced a positive atmosphere within the organization that helped it through tough times and enabled its members to rise to new challenges.

Some leaders might think that Keith's approach was a waste of time. But what Keith instinctively recognized was that if an individual feels acknowledged, and if a team's success is applauded, then the effect on morale and commitment can be significant. For Keith the emphasis on celebration was not a management ploy in order to get the best out of his people. His warm, personal style was natural. He enjoyed expressing thanks. He was good at telling stories. He built on his gifts because he saw the benefit of giving people recognition.

Whenever there was a new project, Keith would be clear about the milestones which could be marked along the way, and he was careful to do this both in writing and orally. Written or emailed notes of thanks and appreciation are always valued, but Keith knew that face-to-face acknowledgement made the offering of thanks more personal and more precious. Telling stories about progress contributes to a sense of achievement. Half way up a mountain, when you look back down the path, you are pleased by the distance you have climbed. It encourages you on as you face the climb ahead.

When Jim leads workshops on subjects such as building resilience or making difficult decisions he starts by asking people in pairs to tell a story about when they had been resilient or when they have made a difficult decision well. Talking through an achievement enables someone to crystallize the approaches and skills that they have used successfully in the past. The workshops then build on this celebration of success to help an individual build on how they are going to grow and guard their resilience or handle difficult decisions more effectively in the future.

Moments of celebration provide a group with a golden opportunity to reflect about what has been achieved, what skills have been developed and what confidences have been enhanced. Celebrations need not be extravagant. They may be based around tea and cakes, or a toast over drinks, or pulling people together for a brief word of thanks. Handwritten thank you notes are worth their weight in gold.

It is easy for a leader who is focused on the future to become obsessive. The danger of only stressing the importance of the onward journey is that we demoralize others. Paradoxically, a key way of galvanizing people about the future is to emphasize what they have achieved. It enhances their self-confidence and motivation. They will then be more likely to demonstrate full commitment to the future without having to be subjected to endless pep talks on the subject. There is a subtlety about motivating people which is rarely about telling them to try harder.

Embarking on a major project can be daunting. But even Everest was climbed one step at a time. When skiing with friends or going on a long distance walk, part of the fun is chunking each day into sections, looking back on what has been achieved and looking forward to the next challenge. We would not countenance setting out on such an adventure without planning ahead, and occasionally pausing for rest and renewal, and yet in our working lives we easily rush on regardless.

It is important, therefore, to help people think of a major project as a sequence of steps. This makes the enterprise manageable and mitigates being overwhelmed by a sense of the nigh impossible. A skilful leader will break down a project into practical steps, and when a milestone has been reached, will use the opportunity to celebrate the achievement. Such celebration is not an indulgence and never a waste of time. It is a crucial acknowledgement of progress and strengthens a sense of shared endeavour. Celebrating what has worked well reinforces the positive and builds enjoyment into what might otherwise be hard grind.

For reflection

- Who in your organization builds a culture of celebration? How do they do it?
- How do you build a culture of celebration into the organization of which you are part?
- How might you link together celebration and reflection in the way you talk with colleagues?
- How might you encourage celebration of success in a way that is genuine and does not come over as 'ticking a box'?

PART FOUR

Read the context

Reflective leaders need to read and interpret the context in which they are operating. To do this well, they will need to immerse themselves in it without becoming dominated by it, lest they lose their perspective or become inhibited from making difficult decisions. They need to grasp the essentials of what is required in the short term without sacrificing strategic thinking about the future to expediency. They have to remain focused in the face of pressure or unrealistic expectations.

This section, therefore, discusses how we can find the right balance between competing claims for our attention. Bringing wisdom to a situation is rarely straightforward. Stress can force even good leaders to make foolhardy or inept decisions. It is important, therefore, to steer a steady course informed by knowledge and intuition, one which distinguishes the important from the merely urgent, and which understands threats but can still take risks. A reflective leader will address the balance between the ideal and the pragmatic, between uncertainty and clarity, and will be free to change direction when and where necessary. The section concludes with an exploration of getting the balance right between giving a lead and enabling others to take a lead in an organization.

22

Maintain the balance between knowledge and wisdom

Bob was clear that he wanted to become head of department in a different school. He enjoyed his work, but wanted the stimulus of a fresh challenge in a new environment. He researched different schools, but each one had its pros and cons. In the end he had amassed so much information that he found himself paralysed in his thinking. He needed wisdom to know where he should throw in his lot.

Finally, a friend helped him stand back and think about what type of staff and young people he would most enjoy working with, and what sort of school atmosphere would be conducive to enable him to flourish. He became clearer about what factors were important to him as he evaluated different options. He was able to make a more informed choice and draft a better job application.

We now have vastly more information at our fingertips than was available to previous generations. We have 24-hour news and the opportunity to search the internet for information on any topic. A wealth of information creates huge opportunities. We can be updated instantly about world events, informed about tomorrow's weather, or read people's opinions on a hotel on the other side of the world. But are we any wiser?

Modern communication can be a power for good. But our unparalleled access to information generates its own pressure. We can become informed quickly about a range of topics, and cannot then justify putting off making a decision on the grounds that we do not have all the information available to us. A wealth of information can paralyse us. We can feel swamped by an abundance of data or so confused by conflicting opinions that we are unable to crystallize our own view.

When a group of leaders was asked about the difference between knowledge and wisdom they said that knowledge was important but insufficient. They described wisdom as the ability to weigh up different options and come to a robust conclusion that stands the test of time. They identified the need to sift painstakingly through information to identify patterns and apply a coherent framework of values. They talked about the importance of standing back from a mass of data to plot the likely consequences of different courses of action. Wisdom draws from the experience of the past, understands human nature well and charts a way forward. Wisdom comes from the synthesis of information with experience.

Each generation likes to think that it is better informed and more enlightened than its predecessor. From our vantage point we look back in horror at how perfectly intelligent people could have supported the slave trade or apartheid, or opposed granting women equal rights. When the history of the beginning of the twenty-first century comes to be written, our descendants will be astonished at how we failed to sort out world poverty when there was more than enough food to go round, or how we consumed so much of the world's resources when we knew perfectly well that such high levels of consumption were unsustainable.

In reality human nature does not change from generation to generation. We may think that we are more enlightened, but the harsh truth is that the twentieth century was the bloodiest century that the world had ever seen. That century saw an arrogant dogmatism that manipulated information to suit political ends. We applaud the fact that today more people have political freedom and free access to information. The peoples of the Baltic States are a good example. However, none of this means that we are necessarily wiser or morally better than our forebears.

When we are faced with a wealth of information, we need to ask ourselves the following questions:

- Which are the significant facts?
- Which trends are the most important?
- What is the range of opinion?
- What can we learn from history? What happened before in similar situations?
- What are likely to be the consequences of what is happening now?

Standing back from a mass of information and reflecting with these types of questions can help put facts into perspective. Some things may seem indisputable, though even then much depends on the eye of the beholder. Different people may challenge us to evaluate information in other ways and allow us to build a more coherent picture about the future.

For example, when a major building project is being considered, the key facts for some people might be the opportunity created by having new accommodation. For others anxiety over the level of disturbance during the construction might be of paramount concern. For others it will be the size of the expenditure and its impact on other priorities. The wisdom to make the right decision will emerge from understanding each person's perspective and being able to assemble the different pieces of the jigsaw into a coherent picture of the project. Information needs to be used to develop a shared understanding, which in turn needs to lead to making wise decisions.

For reflection

- How do you identify key information to build a clear and coherent picture? Who do you normally ask for such information?
- How open are you to the perspectives of others on the same information?
- How can you translate knowledge into wisdom?

23

Maintain the balance between the urgent and the important

Some years ago Judith was required to attend a time management course. In her arrogance, she thought she had little need of such techniques. She was surprised that the course taught her a great deal about herself. Like many of those faced with a few hours at the desk, she sifted through the paperwork and emails and sorted out all the easy problems, kidding herself that she was making progress. By late afternoon she would be left with the two or three most difficult matters unresolved or incomplete.

By this late stage of the day Judith was tired and had used up her creative energy. She postponed making the difficult decision until tomorrow. Judith ended each day knowing that there were some time-consuming and difficult matters that were hanging over her that she would need to deal with the following day. It was not unusual for this same dynamic to go on for weeks.

The time management course helped her see that it was far more effective to identify the most important things that she had to deal with each day and brace herself to resolve them while she was fresh and energized. Once these were completed it felt like a weight was lifted from her which meant that the less important tasks were then completed more quickly.

Few organizations have sufficient staff or resources to do all the things they would like. For most of us there is a pile of unfinished work on the desk at the end of the day. We tend to pick out the jobs that we like doing and put off the ones that we find boring or we think are going to be controversial. We find it easier to be reactive rather than proactive. It is tempting to respond to those who have the loudest voices, so that we can get them off our backs. Meanwhile we hope the other difficult problems will go away. They rarely do.

The ability to prioritize work is a vital discipline if we are going to lead a thriving organization. One of the fundamental aspects of prioritizing is the familiar distinction between the urgent and the important. Urgent matters are the day to day things which are always clamouring for our attention, such as ensuring holiday cover, appointing staff and dealing with disgruntled people.

Important matters are about sustaining the organization for the long term, including initiating new work, spotting emerging trends and bringing on the next generation of workers and leaders. Leaders have to ensure that they give sufficient time to focus on the important issues, rather than always being driven by the urgent issues.

To concentrate on the long-term important issues is one of the most difficult things to do, since it touches on some of our deepest motivations. This is where reflection is essential. We need to recognize the games that we play with ourselves and the avoidance tactics that we sometimes adopt to avoid dealing with the most important things and instead filling our time with fire fighting and handling minutiae.

There are many reasons why leaders put off doing the most important things. Sometimes it is because we know it will create dissension and we would prefer a quiet life. Sometimes it is because we know that we ought to make unpopular decisions and we hate it when people are unhappy with us. At other times it is because we are genuinely unclear about the right decision, so we prevaricate while the underlying problem festers and gets out of hand.

One of the reasons why we tend to concentrate on urgent issues (rather than the important ones) is that we feel that we have achieved something tangible at the end of the day. It is not so demanding to react to what people want from us. However, all the time we are doing this we may not be addressing the long term, underlying issues which are the foundation stones needed to enable the organization to thrive.

The downside of making time to undertake long-term planning is that at the end of the day there may be an even larger pile of urgent matters on the desk. The key is consistent (and persistent) delegation. We have to insist that those around us make the decisions which have been delegated to them. We must not give in to their desire to check everything back with us, thereby refusing to take responsibility.

But there is another reason why prioritizing is vital. If we avoid, either consciously or unconsciously, difficult personnel issues or longer-term questions, we will tend to fill our time with the less important matters. To justify what we do, we will tend to work long hours until we run out of time. When challenged, we justify this by thinking, 'How can I possibly take time out for planning when it is all we can do to get through the immediate work this week?' We then persuade ourselves that it will have to wait until some unspecified time in the future, which never comes.

If we are disciplined in prioritizing and deal with the most essential work, it is easier to stop working earlier. We know that we have dealt with the crucial matters that are our responsibility and which no one else can decide. We can then leave the operational tasks to those who are responsible for that level of the work. Instead of working all the available waking hours and living in a perpetual state of weariness we can enjoy a better balance of time off for rest and recreation.

If our working hours are out of control we are likely to create a culture where everyone feels they must work extra hours to demonstrate their commitment. The consequence may be that they are not delivering what is required because they are too tired and therefore they too are making poor decisions.

For reflection

- Reflect on your current work schedule. How much time do you spend on the urgent and how much on the important?
- How do you assess what are the most important matters that you have to deal with and ensure you concentrate on those?
- How can you avoid getting swamped with urgent matters that take you over? What needs delegating?

24

Maintain the balance between understanding threats and taking risks

Joan saw herself as a naturally cautious person. As a member of the senior executive team of a charity, she was conscious that she had to be mindful of the way resources were spent. Any proposal had to be tried and tested before she would be willing to commit resources to it. But was the charity becoming too restrained? Was it missing opportunities to go into partnership with different organizations? Was it catching the imagination of donors so they were inspired by the innovative work of the charity?

Joan realized that her cautiousness might have gone too far. She had to become more adventurous in her thinking and encourage her colleagues to be bolder so that they might be seen as more up-to-date and relevant. Joan was persuaded that there should be pilot schemes to test out new approaches to both raising resources and spending them effectively. Never one to take great risks, she found herself happily moving into a space where she was becoming more confident in trying out new initiatives.

Joan's story rings true for many of us who prefer to operate in our comfort zone. Our natural tendency is to be cautious. But sometimes we need to break out to grasp new opportunities. A simple method to do this is a SWOT analysis which examines strengths, weaknesses, opportunities and threats. This approach allows strengths and weaknesses to be balanced, and enables opportunities and threats to be viewed alongside each other. Psychologically it is better to consider strengths before weaknesses, and opportunities before threats. Being honest about our weaknesses and the threats puts our strengths and the opportunities into a realistic perspective. What we need to guard against is being overwhelmed by weaknesses or threats. We aim to build on strengths, address our weaknesses, seize the opportunities and minimize the threats.

Because organizations are constantly changing, there are always going to be new opportunities as well as unwelcome threats. A brisk wind can bring sun and showers at frequent intervals. Strong winds of change can mean a buffeting by threats, but may also open up opportunities that we have not had in the past.

When an organization has to reduce its budget significantly, the initial response of employees or volunteers is often disbelief and anger followed by depression and resignation. But tough decisions on funding can lead to more robust prioritizing. Hard questions have to be asked about what investment is working and what is not. Following previous practice is not always a good enough answer.

Tough decisions on funding force individuals to think harder about the benefits of alternative courses of action and the need to work effectively in partnership with others. It might well mean that poor performance gets tackled in a way that had not happened before. It may force us to ask hard questions which should have been addressed earlier.

When a threat has to be faced it is worth asking if there is a silver lining. It is helpful to identify the positive aspects of the situation. For example, ensuring that difficult issues get tackled and, on some occasions, 'naming the elephant', can mean progress is made effectively. Sometimes the opportunities may not be immediately obvious, but at times of change they are always there.

William had always suspected that some of his team members could deliver more. Although they protested that they were working hard, when reductions had to be made in the budget, some members of staff were not replaced. The team reluctantly began to think of different ways of working to cope with the reduction in staffing. Initially, they could see no way forward but their boss asked them repeatedly to reflect and test out new approaches. Eventually, they decided that they could work together in different ways and cut down the time certain processes took. They invested in some new software and were delighted by the difference it made.

Many threats are illusory. Fears about what might go wrong can eat away at our good intentions. The threat of failure, criticism or being derailed may unnerve us. When we feel the technology has let us down, our equilibrium can be disrupted and send us into a downward spiral. We can easily let a threat get to us and destroy our confidence, albeit temporarily.

In response, a practical step is to name the threat, define it, talk it through with someone else and assess it on a scale of one to ten. Threats are best looked at over a period. The strength of a threat depends on whether it is gathering momentum or is a legacy of something that used to be much more severe. An instant judgement about a threat may not give an accurate assessment of its potential impact.

Risks are a necessary evil. Some risks come from external factors, while others we choose to take. If there were no risks life would be dull and boring. There would be no innovation or creativity if we did not explore different avenues. Every time we recommend a course of action we are taking a risk about whether it is likely to work or not.

Living with risk is part of life. Without it we would be very dull leaders. If we are constantly taking huge risks, although it may fascinate or intrigue others, some people may shy away from following us due to fear. Choosing the right risks to take is about careful thought, preparation, evaluation and conversation. The reflective leader weighs up risks carefully and assesses the consequences of alternative courses of action. They have also thought about how to take practical steps to minimize the threats. If no risks are taken, little progress will be made.

For reflection

- What are the threats your organization faces currently?
- How best do you identify them and assess the level of the threat?
- What are the opportunities that might open up for you? What new opportunities might you pursue over the next year?
- What calculated risks are you prepared to take over the next few days as a leader?

25

Maintain the balance between the ideal and the pragmatic

Nicholas was appointed chief executive of a major charity. He was keen to encourage it to develop a new initiative among disadvantaged young people in inner city areas. He had undertaken a great deal of research and was clear that there was an urgent need to stimulate an innovative social inclusion programme. He also believed that there was scope to build a donor base to support such a move. His ideal was clear and there were some who shared his passion. However, what surprised him was the level of donor resistance to sponsoring projects outside the charity's traditional remit. The board of trustees was reluctant to move even into an exploratory stage or pilot one or two projects.

Nicholas was unwilling to give up, but recognized that he also needed to be pragmatic. He abandoned his initial timetable as unrealistic. He recognized that he had to build his case for development step by step, starting with a pilot project supported by three or four key donors, to explore the potential benefits of a new approach and the extent to which it was attractive to donors.

Ideals motivate us. The challenge of climbing to the top of a mountain galvanizes our energies. Setting out on a journey towards an exciting destination focuses our minds. We need to re-examine our ideals regularly. Are they based on the values that matter most to us? Are they consistent with what is intellectually, ethically and spiritually important to us? Do our ideals make it worth getting up in the morning?

None of us has an unlimited amount of time or energy. We have to make choices. If we are clear something is a second order issue, then it may be in our own best interests in terms of health and effectiveness to walk away from it. We can then free ourselves and our energies to concentrate on the more important matters. It is not indulgent to reflect on the outcomes that are most important to us. This is a necessary part of refreshing our clarity of purpose. An ideal that is completely irrelevant or wholly unobtainable is self-delusory. An ideal that might just be attainable can motivate and take us into new and exciting opportunities. A key test is to ask if the ideal is rooted in reality.

The cautionary advice is sometimes given, 'Be careful what you wish for'. When we have an ideal about say, leading a project in Africa, we may spot opportunities that we would not have previously recognized. Although we may feel it is foolhardy to share such an ambition, we may discover that once others know our plans they will want to work with us to make them happen.

Producing an ideal outcome is a worthy aspiration, but sometimes the 'best can be the enemy of the good'. Striving for excellence is important but if we always seek absolute perfection we may need to ask whether we are using our time appropriately. The senior teacher has to share their time between all their staff. Their ideal may be to spend an hour a week mentoring each person who reports directly to them. But that is not realistic and choices have to be made. At one point it may be more important to give support to a teacher who is clearly struggling. At other times we may need to invest in a teacher who has great untapped potential, enabling them to take on more responsibilities.

This is why our ideals need to be tempered with pragmatism. However, pragmatism without ideals can be stultifying and boring. Indeed, if it crosses the line with expediency, ideals can easily go out of the window. But when our ideals are earthed in realism, then we are likely to identify an exciting and practical way forward.

Pragmatism may feel like a poor second best. We have had to accept an outcome that is less than our ideal. It can feel like being tainted with compromise. Nevertheless, reflecting on the link between the principles we most aspire to and the pragmatic route we have chosen is important. Knowing and recognizing the relationship between the ideal and the pragmatic gives an equilibrium that is essential for survival.

Lithuania is a country whose people celebrate their freedom and independence in the twenty-first century. They are now able to live out their ideal of an independent state. The country has been occupied at various times by the Poles, the French, the Nazis and the Soviets, yet their ideal to be an independent people has lived on. They have had to be pragmatic at times and live within alien regimes. Some of the beautifully restored churches in Vilnius, the capital of Lithuania, are a tribute to the resilience of a people who have lived through much pain over recent centuries and have kept their ideal to be an independent people determining their own future.

As a leader, being pragmatic is about taking one step at a time. It is being clear what is achievable and what progress can be made through consensus at a particular time. It is about keeping people on board so that they accept and recognize the progress that has been made. Every long journey starts with one step. The ability to walk a long way depends on seeing how far you have come, recognizing progress and seeing where the journey might lead. Pragmatism can become a 'world weariness' which overwhelms our ideals. Sometimes a reconnection with the ideal, for example, through a conversation with a younger person can be invigorating.

Having an ideal sustains motivation, although we may be 'in the wilderness for 40 years' before the destination is reached. Being pragmatic will include recognizing our limitations and the need for patience. It may be some time before a clear view about the right destination emerges.

The reflective leader keeps the ideal in mind, continually

revisiting it in the light of experience. They take people along with them in a pragmatic way, allowing them to own and to modify the ideal. As a result there is a strong sense of walking together to the same drumbeat.

For reflection

- How have you balanced the ideal and pragmatic in the recent past? Would you make the same decision if you were revisiting that situation?
- How will you balance the ideal and the pragmatic in a future choice?
- How do you ensure that when you are pragmatic, you are not taking the easy way out?

26

Maintain the balance between uncertainty and clarity

The company where Helen worked was going through a period of turbulence. The turnover figures had gone down and costs had to be cut. She did not feel as motivated as she had done a year ago. What turned the atmosphere around? John, the senior manager of her unit, addressed issues openly in a sequence of staff meetings. He shared the uncertainties, explained the reasons for them and set out some perspectives about the next steps. He also encouraged constructive conversation about the type of contribution which members of staff could make.

Quietly and carefully, John took the teams through the issues and encouraged them to contribute their perspectives. It now became a shared problem and not just something that was being imposed on them. John's reflective approach, in talking through the uncertainties, helped Helen and her colleagues to be thoughtful about the future and keep up their levels of motivation. As the recession eased, the company was well equipped to take advantage of new opportunities.

So often we think of uncertainty as a threat. We only see the dark side of what might happen. We become encircled in gloom with our optimism gone and our motivation sapped. But uncertainty can sometimes be a gift. It can force us to stand back and reflect on what is most important and what we want to see happen. Uncertainty can create a climate where people are more willing to listen and explore different avenues. We all like a degree of certainty, but if everything is predictable, we are less likely to be creative and innovative.

Uncertainty can provide the stimulus to think in new and different ways. It gives us an incentive to find out how other people are tackling similar challenges. It can make us open-minded and recognize that the world will not always be as we currently know it. Perhaps we should celebrate uncertainty rather than be worried by it?

In the story above John addressed the uncertainty by being open with his team and encouraging them to reflect together. If he had tried to be dogmatically optimistic his team might not have believed him. The approach that worked was to allow each member of the team to voice their uncertainties, assess the range of options and think constructively about the best way to move forward. So often we think that expressing uncertainty is a sign of weakness. In reality, it takes a strong leader to talk about the principles that will be used to address the uncertainties and the approaches that will be adopted to test out next steps.

Living with uncertainty is a fact of life. Sometimes, having undertaken all the research that is possible and having consulted those who might have a considered opinion, we have not yet identified what we think is the best course of action. Indeed, there may not be a right way forward, only two options, neither of which we particularly like. It is at this point that uncertainty can paralyse us.

When uncertainty is in danger of gripping us, practical steps include:

- Reflect on how you have dealt with uncertainty effectively in the past.
- Seek the perspective of others who have been in similar situations.
- Go back to first principles that have been behind the success of the organization so far.

- Be utterly objective about the issues that are being faced and address them one step at a time.
- Create space where, along with others in the organization, you can reflect about the uncertainties.

In a calm, measured atmosphere, progress might be made by addressing key questions such as:

- Is there anything important about the background we do not know enough about?
- Are there any trends that we have not fully explored?
- Are there other factors we should reflect on?
- What questions have we not yet asked because we have not fully appreciated their importance?

Living through uncertainty requires holding our nerve when those around us are going into denial. It can be about recognizing that the mist comes and goes. Sometimes it is not possible to see far ahead, and then suddenly there is clarity about the way forward. It can mean saying that we need to have a steady hand on the tiller and keep going on a pre-planned course of action which has been well researched.

Addressing uncertainty may involve saying that now is not the moment. There will be a time when a decision needs to be taken; when the fog has cleared a bit. We will probably be aware when that point has been reached, but now we have to live through uncertainty and accept that not every issue can be resolved at the time of our choosing.

Barbara was one of the leaders of a charity which needed to face up to a health and safety issue. In a time of financial stringency, extra expenditure was needed to provide access for wheelchair users. There was some scepticism about whether the expenditure was justified. Barbara did not waver but kept the matter on the agenda. She continued to reflect with colleagues about the clear case for the expenditure and the consequences of not taking action.

Eventually, there was acquiescence. When the project was completed there was a general recognition that it had been worth doing and that Barbara was right to ensure there was clarity about the necessity of action. Barbara had to lead through other people's uncertainty which she did with calm persistence. She drew on the support of two or three friends who helped her reflect on how best to deal with this uncertainty and hold her nerve.

For reflection

- Can you think back to a time of uncertainty in your work? What was good about the way the leader dealt with it? How might it have been handled even more effectively?
- What are the fixed points for you when you are uncertain?
- How can you enable other people to work through their own uncertainties?

27

Maintain the balance between giving clear direction and willingness to change

Hazel was a college lecturer. She wanted to impart information and wisdom to her students, and had refined her lecture notes over many years. Hazel continued to add up-to-date examples to illustrate her material, but attendance at her lectures had begun to dwindle. Her students were not as engaged as in times past. Hazel found this apparent disengagement difficult to understand.

Some of Hazel's students, in a gentle way, suggested to her that they were now used to a more participative style of learning. Hazel decided to adopt a different approach. She broke the students into small groups. She involved them more by using questions and asking them to express their opinions. She then began to experiment in her main teaching groups and found, to her surprise, that the students responded well.

Hazel divided her material into sections. She encouraged the students to think about different approaches. She made it clear that she expected them to contribute more in the teaching groups. Hazel used her wisdom and knowledge to summarize and steer conversations rather than lecture at her students. The fact that she could change her approach, and the positive reception she received from the students, was an encouragement to Hazel. Her one regret was that she should have changed her approach years earlier.

For many people the traditional image of the leader is some-body who instructs others what to do. Helen's style had been to tell her students what to think and to give them directions. Her approach worked up to a point but did not bring out the best in them.

There are occasions when it is essential for a leader to give a command. The captain in a sports team has to decide the next move, and for it to work well everyone has to follow the instruction. In a crisis a leader has to take control and give orders about what is to happen next. There may be a few minutes' consultation, but then instructions need to be set out succinctly, with clarity about who is responsible to implement them. Leaders need to be able to give a clear sense of direction. If we are going to follow, we want to know where the leader is taking us. If we are to be motivated to follow the direction someone has set, we may need to be convinced that the leader has thought it through and knows the way forward.

However, most of us respect a leader who is willing to change direction when they have been persuaded that there is a better way forward. We are cautious about a leader who seems blinkered to new information or changed reality. The leader who unremittingly articulates their case without devia-tion can be inspiring initially, but then the repetition becomes a source of suspicion. If someone is so fixed in their views and their language, how can they be listening to those around them and be mindful of the changing context or expectations?

A leader who has inspired us by their clear sense of direction, can reinforce the confidence we have in them if that clarity is balanced by reflection. The individual who is willing to spend time away from the heat of the moment assessing whether the direction they have set needs modifying, builds rather than diminishes the respect of those they have a responsibility to lead.

Some leaders feel that they have to demonstrate that they are a step ahead of everyone else, that they know all the answers and that they are able to take the best decisions in any circumstance. They fear that if they change their mind, it will be seen as an act of weakness or even desperation. Leaders need to be self-confident enough in themselves to be able to admit, either that they were wrong, or that there is now a better course of action to be taken.

A leader may make poor decisions if they are always trying to prove something to themselves and others. Wanting to be a step ahead of others is commendable in terms of planning, but it is dangerous if the leader feels compelled to put a personal stamp on the way forward. Far better is the desire to empower others to think ahead too so there is a joint endeavour about what comes next.

The ideal is to bring a level of maturity that enables us to set out our preferred approach, listen carefully to others and acknowledge when we have changed our mind. A leader who is explicit that they will be open minded, will listen to alternatives, and adopt a different solution if a better one is proposed, builds huge credibility by their willingness to engage.

A good way of creating a culture of reflection in an organization is for the leader to show that they are open to new ideas or different ways of thinking. This is also encouraged when a leader acknowledges how their original proposal has been modified to respond to current events. The leader who is seen to reflect, take in new information and perspectives, and re-evaluate and redefine their approach will stimulate the same behaviours within their organization. There is a natural tendency in any organization to emulate the approach of the leader.

Allied to an open mindedness to change direction is the importance of two-way communication. Many of us resent being told what to think. We respect those who carefully explain their perspective and how it has changed, but then allow us to reach our own conclusions. Effective reflection is not only about how we reach conclusions, it is also about the pace and style in which these are communicated. It is important that the hearer understands and accepts the reasons at both an emotional as well as a rational level and is, therefore, more willing to change their approach.

For reflection

- Reflect on your style of leadership. Do you tend to issue instructions or work consensually? Are you clear when one style is more appropriate than the other?
- Can you think of an example when you changed your mind recently? What did you learn from this?
- Who are your sounding boards when you think that you might need to change your mind?

28

Maintain the balance between giving a lead and enabling others to take the lead

Barry held an influential position in the organization in which he worked. He rarely gave direct instructions in an authoritarian manner but instead developed the skill of dropping ideas or suggestions into conversations. Because people trusted his perspective they would seek his views. He was highly skilled at asking the right questions and setting an individual off to reflect on different ideas.

As a board member he had the power of direction, but used it sparingly. He had learnt that the best way to motivate people was to put them in a position where they developed their own actions rather than being told what to do. He knew how to provide a framework and a perspective which meant that the ideas individuals and teams developed fitted with the overall strategy of the organization. When he retired he was greatly missed because of his positive influence which enabled people to think in new and constructive ways.

Barry's skill as a leader was to be selective about when he set out a particular direction. As a member of the organization's executive board he had ensured that there was a clear, overall strategy within which he and others were operating. There was then a lot of freedom to decide how those priorities were achieved. Barry knew from years of experience that the best ideas result from individuals and teams working through

issues with energy and passion. Barry concentrated on foster-
ing a culture where this happened. He expected colleagues
to think hard about different options and to reflect clearly
and purposefully. He did not believe in giving his employees
instructions on tablets of stone. Instead, he shared stories and
posed questions that stimulated others to think in fresh and
creative ways.

The effective leader uses a wide repertoire of approaches
which includes questioning, suggesting, influencing, persuading and sometimes directing. An arrogant leader asks one
demanding question after another which is guaranteed to kill
any sense of common purpose or joint endeavour. A good
question is followed by space allowing the hearers to think
through their response. There needs to be a sense of shared
engagement leading to a solution to which all parties can
be committed. Any leader wanting to take forward a major
initiative needs to build a common understanding of the
benefits of the project. The leader might have their own personal views but other key people will need to help shape the
outcome so they are fully committed to the action needed to
get there.

Getting the right results in terms of the specification for a
major project is rarely about the leader saying, 'this is what
is going to happen'. It involves a lot of hard work, thinking
through options and consulting with those who are going to
be affected. We have to examine all the possible consequences
of each decision and consider which partnerships are likely to
be sustainable. Adjustments will be necessary along the way
and reaching consensus will normally require time. Rushing decisions can lead to barriers going up and fixed views
re-emerging. Consensus is often found a step at a time with
progress needing to be acknowledged at each stage.

Final responsibility usually rests with one person, for
example the chief executive, managing partner or bishop.
Sometimes, decisions cannot be and should not be made by
consensus. In a crisis it is the responsibility of the leader to
decide what action is going to be taken. Reasons can and

should be given afterwards, but in the moment decisiveness is paramount.

Taking overall responsibility as a leader can be a lonely experience. Others may have been happy for you to become the leader, but there is bound to be unease or criticism when you take decisions which they find difficult to accept. You may feel that people become distanced from you, which is perhaps inevitable in some cases. Reflective leaders do not shirk from the responsibilities placed on them, but try to build as much agreement as possible about the way forward. This necessitates being clear about the next steps. Creating space for others to accept and understand why a decision has been made is highly desirable so that any unease is minimized.

As a leader Jesus was a remarkable example of someone who varied his repertoire of approaches. Sometimes he made direct challenges or exhortations. On other occasions he used stories or memorable sayings to stimulate the thinking of his followers. He used the apprentice model: 'You have seen me do it, now you go and do the same.' At other times he gave a clear steer to his disciples and enabled them to grow through their experiences until they were equipped to lead the church.

It is easy to underestimate the power of influence. If, as a leader, we build up trust we can create a strong desire for people to want to talk to us and hear our views. This in turn enables us to be a significant source of influence through suggestion. If, through the use of stories and illustrations, we help others reflect on what might be possible, we may develop their leadership skills way beyond their expectations.

For reflection

- When have you not got the balance quite right between giving a lead and enabling others to take the lead? What did you learn from this experience?

- When were you at your most influential during the last month? Why were you influential?
- How can you use the power of the question to encourage and enable individuals to lead more effectively?
- How might you use stories or reflections to help stimulate the thinking of others?

PART FIVE

Next steps

As you have read this book and reflected on your leadership style and skills, you will have grown in self-understanding. Hopefully you will have gained deeper insights about your colleagues and the dynamics of the team. We hope you will have a greater awareness of the context in which you are currently working.

So what next? Perhaps the first twenty-eight reflections and the concluding questions have sparked off new thoughts or confirmed some of your previous perspectives.

We conclude with three chapters which might give you pause for thought as you consider further what being a reflective leader means for you.

- What happens when you stand and stare?
- What lights your fire?
- Who are your companions on the way?

Being a reflective leader requires an acute sense of observation to read what is going on around you. It also requires an awareness of what lights your fire and the willingness to see your passions reignited. Essential to thriving as a reflective leader is having good companions who will encourage, support and challenge you.

29

What happens when you stand and stare?

Joel could not stop. His brain was always rushing ahead. As soon as one problem had been solved, he was on to the next challenge. He enjoyed this relentless pursuit of activity, although sometimes it exhausted him. It certainly tired those around him who had stopped trying to keep up with him long ago.

Life was about constant rushing with little time for reflection or observation. Joel felt like the long-distance runner out on his own at the front of the pack, both pleased with himself for his athletic prowess but wanting the encouragement of fellow runners. Sometimes he could be quite lonely.

After one busy week, exhaustion hit Joel. It came like a thud to the stomach with the sensation of being bent over and unable to stand upright to face the world confidently. He had to rest, and it was a few weeks before his energy returned. Gradually, he got back into his stride. He was both frustrated by his slow recovery, and also thankful that he was now becoming more observant about himself and others. The experience slowed him down. Just occasionally, he would stand and stare and a wry smile would come over his face, recollecting how resistant he had previously been to stopping and listening.

Taking time out to stand and stare can make us feel guilty. The energy and passion that led to our appointment as a leader did not come from hanging around doing nothing. We fear it is an indulgence to pause, even though we can be remarkably good at telling other people to slow down. We may be eloquent and use cogent arguments to cajole a family member or friend who is overworking to ease up. We are delighted when we help someone else slow down, but do not readily recognize it when we ourselves are working manically. Maybe we see the speck in someone else's eye more readily than the log in our own.

To stand and stare is to observe, to be ready to see the unexpected, to enjoy the ordinary and predictable, to observe the rhythms of human behaviour and be enthralled or amused by them. It may involve watching a baby rolling on the floor, or a toddler building a tower. For others it is about standing on the touchline watching a game of hockey, or observing the stars in the night sky with a group of friends. When we stand and stare with those we know and love, we are uplifted by their companionship and friendship. There is a mutuality of emotional embrace and humour. The laughter is deep and not superficial.

Simply spending an extra five minutes at a viewpoint soaking up the colours and the patterns in the landscape can be transformative. It might mean staying out on the deck of a boat, even when we become cold, to observe the wind and the waves, and to see the light as it reflects on the rocks and bounces on the water. It can be rejuvenating when we soak up the natural environment. We can be uplifted by the wonder and richness of the created order.

To stand and stare might be to read some thought-provoking words in a book or article for a second time. It may come from some inspiring words of poetry. It could be an idea that we let float in our mind which we then observe from different standpoints in order to think about its implications and insights. Our natural tendency might be to rush from one thought to another, but mulling an idea over can help put it into a wider context and enable us to think in depth rather than with shallowness about issues we face in our community or nation.

To stand and stare is about nurturing the spiritual side of our lives, as well as attending to our emotional and intellectual well-being. All of us need to integrate our beliefs, our hopes and our fears, and to focus on what is truly important to us. Such moments of quietness, when we reflect on what matters most, are vital if we are to keep our lives in equilibrium. They also allow us to identify where we want to make a difference in life.

Carving out time for personal reflection is not always easy. It can mean pursuing thoughts and ideas to a deeper level, which can shake us out of our comfortable assumptions. But the hard work of exploring new ideas can be rewarding. It can set us off in a fresh direction with renewed energy and purpose.

How best do we create space to stand and stare? Some practical steps might be:

- Standing an extra five minutes in a place we enjoy, soaking up the atmosphere.
- Deliberately observing those around us, looking at their faces and imagining their thoughts.
- Observing some aspects of the created order and enjoying the beauty in the bird, flower, mountain or piece of grass.
- Letting time go slowly through breathing deeply and blanking out of our minds the pressures that can overwhelm us.
- Turning off all electronic means of communication to create some quiet space.
- Looking for the ridiculous in what we observe and allowing ourselves to smile.
- Considering what stand and stare techniques work best for us, and being disciplined to cultivate them.

Above all, banish the notion that to stand and stare is to waste time and is an indulgence. It can give us new energy and helps us put the pressures of the day into a wider perspective. Renewed by some moments of calm, it will put back a spring in our step.

For reflection

- When did you recently stand and stare? What do you remember most about the experience?
- When might you stand and stare more often? How can you ensure this happens?
- How can other people help you feel good about times when you stand and stare?

30

What lights your fire?

Roger had enjoyed his working life in the accounts department at a local factory. He valued his colleagues and found satisfaction in doing a job well. But in recent years his work had seemed less fulfilling as more responsibility had moved to others. It had become repetitive and he was happy to move on.

When Roger retired he was asked if he would become a trustee of a local housing charity. Slightly half-heartedly he agreed. It turned out to be the best decision he had made in years. He saw at first hand the issues of human poverty the charity was addressing. Roger was inspired by what they were seeking to achieve. His work with the charity became a highlight of the week. His new energy was obvious to his family and friends as his responsibilities with the charity had 'lit his fire'.

If we do not pause and reflect, we may find ourselves rushing around in many different directions. There is a danger that we become boringly predictable and completely exhausting to others. On the other hand, if doing nothing is our favourite activity we may become dull and inconsequential. Too much introspective reflection can send us into a downward spiral when the energy goes out of us and we bump along achieving little.

Self-reflection is valuable in understanding where we are coming from and what our concerns are. It can make us aware of our innermost hopes and fears. A period of quiet inner reflection can help us put our concerns into proportion. The awareness of what lights our fire is a precious gift. If we are ablaze with energy all the time we would burn ourselves to a cinder. The flames of energy would mean there is a risk of our being singed by the heat – or make the glue that holds life together melt and drip away.

Many different elements can light our fire: the passions that are important to us; the areas where we want to make a difference in life; the people in whose company we feel encouraged and inspired; the activities which make us feel good about ourselves and the world around us; a time of quiet or retreat; the conversations which raise our hopes and expectations; and the physical activities that give us a sense of energy. Lighting the fire within us is not about preoccupation with ourselves. It is about recognizing what gives us energy and vitality. It is acknowledging that some people and situations are sapping, while other people and situations energize us.

If going for a run lights your fire, can you do more of it? If reading a Jane Austen novel, or a Shakespearian play or a book by a famous author or watching Shrewsbury Town Football Club lights your fire, can you find time to do it more frequently? This is about being indulgent in an activity that gives you energy that is not detrimental to others. The energy we possess is not finite. It can vary depending on the situation we are in, the people we are with, our understanding of ourselves and our appreciation of the contribution that we can make in our community or the wider world.

William Wilberforce wrote about, 'being diligent in the business of life'. This gave him a sense of purpose and energy in his determination to end the slave trade in the United Kingdom 200 years ago. Having a sense of purpose linked to making a difference in our family, community or work can have a significant effect on our energy levels and on our physical, intellectual, emotional and spiritual well-being.

At various stages of life different activities will light our fire. In our thirties and forties it might be spending time with children and young people. In our fifties and sixties it might be involvement in a church, charity or community group giving back to society and helping to light the fire of other people.

What lights our fire may change over time. Our background or an early life discouragement, may mean that experiences or perspectives are buried deep within us. What might be practical steps that will help you light your fire? These might include:

- Being explicit about what gives me energy, and what circumstances sap my energy.
- Spending time with people who stimulate us. Making sure that time with these people stays in our diary.
- Recognizing what we are passionate about and being wary about those who quench our passions.
- Always asking ourselves where we can make a positive difference within our family, our community or our sphere of work.
- When we are low or tired remembering what can 'light our fire' and raise our energy levels.
- Banishing the notion that it is indulgent to think about what will light our fire.

For reflection

- Who do you value spending time with who helps light your fire and energizes you?
- What type of situation do you want to put yourself in over the next few weeks which you know will light your fire?
- What ideas are flickering at the moment about where you can contribute and make a positive difference for good?

Who are your companions
on the way

> Dietrich loved going for long walks. He relished the smells and vistas of a hike through the countryside. A joy for him was being able to look back and see the route he had taken and observe the landscape he had walked through.
>
> Part of the pleasure of walking alone was having spontaneous conversations with other walkers. His companions on the way were sometimes young and energetic. At other times he walked with older hikers who were taking the journey at a slower pace. He enjoyed the camaraderie of talking about the route, the weather or the trees. Sometimes the conversation could be more serious as people shared stories about their work and their lives. After walking with someone for a couple of hours, Dietrich knew what made them tick and why the long walk appealed to them.
>
> Whenever he went on a hike, Dietrich would look out for new companions. He was always interested in people and wanted to learn by building an understanding of their hopes and joys, their histories and their sadnesses. Having good companions on the way helped Dietrich reflect on his own journey and what mattered most to him.

Our companions on the way may be those we know well and with whom we have journeyed together through different aspects of life's experience. Many things can be unspoken with friends of long-standing where there is a richness of shared experience. Seeing a friend after a period of absence can mean a renewed buzz as we slip back into a deep level of rapport and conversation quickly. It is as if we last saw that person the day before rather than the year before.

Such companions on the way can help us reflect. Many people find that new ideas and opportunities have arisen when we have been in conversation with old friends. Having talked through our hopes and fears, we come to a clearer understanding about the next steps on our journey. Treasured companions are a deep source of gentle prompting to help us reflect constructively in a way which is rooted in our experience and values, and open to change and new insights.

It can be good to reflect on:

- Who are the companions on our way who have been most influential upon us? What was it about them that made them so influential upon us?
- Who helps us reflect in a way that is both energizing and helps us link with the values, beliefs and purposes that are most important to us?
- In what physical space do we have the best conversations with friends?
- What might we do over the next few weeks to meet up with companions and to reflect on the next steps of our journey?

Conversing with companions requires flexibility and reciprocity. It may well be that one person's need to reflect will be greater at one time than another. Give and take will be vital for companionship to remain fresh, continuous and growing. Recognizing the phases in friendship is essential to its future health.

Having good companions on the way is not just about being with friends. It is also about being open to conversations with new people in different contexts. Part of the delight of being a human being is the ability to communicate through listening, observing and talking with people from different backgrounds and cultures. Some of the most valuable and worthwhile friendships are those which cross cultural boundaries. Being alert to the way new conversations go, and enlivened by that sense of hope and fun that comes out of such discussions, can renew our passion for living and for the future.

Who might be our new companions on the way? How might we engage with:

- People who have interesting ideas and perspectives?
- Individuals who have similar interests or work experiences to us?
- Individuals we meet at social, community or church events who are living and working in a different context but with whom there are shared values and interests.

How might we communicate a sense of joy and encouragement to those people we meet very briefly in our daily work or travel? How can we enable friends and acquaintances when they finish a conversation with us to feel energized and glad they had talked with us?

Often we need our own space to reflect. At other times we need the stimulus of others to bring the best out of us. Some of us only know what we think when we hear ourselves say it. Others of us do our best thinking in quiet with no one else getting in the way. Our own self-awareness is at the heart of our understanding of when we need companions along the way and how best we enjoy and are enriched by others.

For reflection

- Who are the companions who help you reflect best?
- Who might you like to build a stronger sense of rapport with, in order to build more shared reflection time?
- How might you be more open to new companions on the way and to the richness which comes from reflecting with new people?

Postscript

We hope that these chapters and the questions at the end of each chapter have given you food for thought. We trust that the book has set you off thinking in a slightly different way or encouraged you to take a particular action.

It might have enabled you to understand yourself better in terms of your core values and motivations. You may have gained insights into others, and what motivates or paralyses them. Perhaps it will have stimulated you to think about how best you can enable teams to grow and excel. It might have given you the framework to look at the wider context in a rapidly changing world to help you address some of the dilemmas that we all face.

Whatever issues the book has raised, allow yourself the time to reflect and begin to enjoy a greater sense of clarity about your own next steps. Sometimes reflection is about enjoying the stillness and understanding yourself and your motivations better. Making time for reflection can lead to greater clarity about what you believe is important and the people, passions and places that are special to you. It can be about allowing yourself to be a quiet influence for good enriching others through bringing love, joy, peace, patience, kindness, goodness, faithfulness, gentleness and self-control, which are some of the consequences of quiet reflection.

In your busy life, allow yourself to stand still so you can move forward.

Other books written by
Alan Smith and Peter Shaw

Alan Smith

Growing up in Multifaith Britain: explorations in youth, ethnicity and religion, Cardiff: University of Wales Press, 2007

God-Shaped Mission: theological and practical perspectives from the rural church, Norwich: Canterbury Press, 2008

Peter Shaw

Mirroring Jesus as Leader, Cambridge: Grove, 2004

Conversation Matters: how to engage effectively with one another, London: Continuum, 2005

The Four Vs of Leadership: Vision, Values, Value-added and Vitality, Chichester: Capstone, 2006

Finding Your Future: the second time around, London: Darton Longman and Todd, 2006

Business Coaching: achieving practical results through effective engagement, Chichester: Capstone, 2007. (Co-authored with Robin Linnecar)

Making Difficult Decisions: how to be decisive and get the business done, Chichester: Capstone, 2008

Deciding Well: a Christian Perspective on making decisions as a Leader, Vancouver: Regent College Publishing, 2009

Raise Your Game: how to succeed at work, Chichester: Capstone, 2009

Effective Christian Leaders in the Global Workplace, Colorado Springs: Authentic/Paternoster, 2010

Defining Moments: Navigating through Business and Organisational Life, Basingstoke: Palgrave/Macmillian, 2010

Forthcoming books

Thriving in your Work, London: Marshall Cavendish, 2011

Effective Leadership Teams: A Christian Perspective, London: Darton Longman and Todd, 2012 (Co-authored with Judy Hirst)